SUSTAINABLE EXCELLENCE

TEN PRINCIPLES TO LEADING YOUR
UNCOMMON AND EXTRAORDINARY LIFE

TERRY TUCKER

Five
Stones
Press

COPYRIGHT

Library of Congress Control Number 2020917195
ISBN-13 : 978-1951129521 (Hardcover edition)

First Edition

Cover Design: Wicked Smart Designs
Editorial Team: Imogen Howsen, Kimberly Cannon & Ava Hodge
Interior Formatting: Five Stones Press Design Team
Publisher: Five Stones Press, Dallas, Texas

For quantity sales, textbooks, and orders by trade bookstores or wholesalers contact Five Stones Press at publish@fivestonespress.net

Five Stones Press is owned and operated by Five Stones Church, a nonprofit 501c3 religious organization. Press name and logo are trademarked. Contact publisher for use.

Terry Tucker's author website is motivationalcheck.com.

Printed in the United States of America

DEDICATION

To my wife Roberta and our daughter Mikela, for loving me, supporting me, and caring for me. I have so much love and gratitude in my soul for you both and appreciate you showing me how to live an uncommon and extraordinary life.

PRAISE FOR SUSTAINABLE EXCELLENCE

"Terry Tucker has given all readers of Sustainable Excellence an uncommon and extraordinary gift. The meaningful stories of his life experiences as a police officer, basketball player, father, husband, friend, and ten-year cancer patient will change lives for the better. His ten principles provide practical and engaging insights to find purpose, to live being uncomfortable, to take responsibility for your life, to handle life's setbacks, and to never give up. It is a very enjoyable read, including lessons from Dr. Seuss and Curious George! As we confront the major challenges of a pandemic, racial injustice, and economic instability, Sustainable Excellence will provide needed support and guidance on how to live our lives with meaning and purpose."

Nancy M. Schlichting
Former President and CEO, Henry Ford Health System, Detroit,
Michigan
Author, Unconventional Leadership

I have known Terry Tucker my whole life. He is a man of principle that has overcome more challenges than any person should be presented in multiple lifetimes. There is no better role model for leading and teaching us how we can live our uncommon and extraordinary life.

Gene Henneberry,
President and CEO, SMBC Rail

An inspiring read that spoke to me just when I needed to hear Terry's message! Life perspectives offered by a gentleman who has truly lived and loved what he challenges us all to create, an uncommon and extraordinary life. Don't be afraid to dive into his book and emerge motivated to go for it. All for the greater praise and glory of God.

Colleen D. Mitchell,
Founder, VENTURE 3PHILANTHROPY

CONTENTS

INTRODUCTION

When fabled Green Bay Packers football coach, Vince Lombardi, took over the fledgling team, he said this to his players: "Gentleman, we will chase perfection, and we will chase it relentlessly, knowing all the while we can never attain it. But along the way, we will catch excellence."

But what is excellence, and how do we know when we have achieved it? Numerous synonyms describe the ethereal word *excellence*: outstanding, brilliant, high quality, indispensable, or extremely good. We look at profitable companies with unique cultures, or successful artists who relentlessly slave at their craft, or difference-makers who attempt to positively change the world, as being excellent in their field.

The Greek philosopher Aristotle defined excellence as "a mean between two extremes of excess and defect in regard to a feeling or action as the practically wise person would determine it." According to Aristotle, a "mean" cannot be calculated and is relative to the individual and circumstances. To Aristotle, excellence was defined by the person and the conditions under which it was viewed. So, excellence, like beauty, tends to be in the eye of the beholder.

People love lists. When David Letterman was the host of the popular television show *Late Night* he always had a "Top Ten List" segment in the show. I've heard many reasons why lists are so popular. Things like: "Because we are constantly bombarded with information, we become overstimulated, and lists provide us with continuity." Or: "A list of topics provides our brains with decisiveness and definitiveness." Or my favorite: "Lists provide us with a form of communication that allows us to know exactly what we are getting."

Every Monday morning, on my website, Motivational Check, I publish the Monday Morning Motivational Message. This message is one of the most popular segments on the site. While many of these messages are short stories that teach a lesson, I get the highest positive feedback when I post a list of something. The topic of the lists doesn't usually matter; what matters to the readers is that they have an inventory that purports to improve their lives.

In early 2020, I had a recent college graduate connect with me on LinkedIn. The thing that drew my attention to this young man was a question he asked me. He wanted to know what I thought were the "most important lessons" he needed to succeed.

As I considered how I wanted to respond to him, I thought back to my college days at The Citadel in Charleston, South Carolina, and some of the most important lessons I learned about leadership, excellence, and myself.

I was fortunate to accept a basketball scholarship to attend The Citadel, The Military College of South Carolina, in 1978. I had received no formal training in leadership up until this point in my life. My parents had modeled what good behavior should look like and set an example of how I should treat others. Still, I didn't fully understand what leadership or excellence meant until I attended The Citadel.

As I quickly grabbed a piece of paper and began jotting down lessons I have learned over my sixty years in my roles as husband, father, police officer, hostage negotiator, basketball coach, business owner, and most recently, cancer warrior, the words, "the most important lessons" this young man wanted to know, stuck in my mind. I didn't want the list to be the generic, "work hard," "be polite," "help others," etc. I didn't want to give him a catalog of rules, or canons, or directives. I wanted my responses to be deeper, more profound, and worthy of putting in the time to make them part of who he was and who he wanted to become. I wanted to develop principles that would help this young man become unstoppable at his craft, but I wanted the list to ensure that he could sustain excellence, once it was achieved.

I sought to provide him with a list of principles rooted in bedrock to form the foundation of unshakable beliefs and dedicated behaviors despite the prodigious and tumultuous circumstances that he might encounter during his life.

I remember one of the stories that I often tell when I am interviewed on a podcast, or speak to groups. The story is about the scene in the movie *Rocky*, where Rocky guzzles the five raw eggs.

Whenever I tell this story, I ask the audience to put themselves in the place of Rocky and apply the scene to defining their brand of excellence.

As a prelude to the scene, Rocky is a two-bit pugilist who has no hopes of ever making it big in the boxing world. His job is to collect the outstanding debts for the neighborhood loan shark.

However, out of the blue, Rocky is chosen to fight the heavyweight champion of the world, Apollo Creed. Rocky doesn't have a manager or a trainer. To prepare for the fight, he develops his unique style of training. This scene is the beginning of Rocky's battle to get himself in shape for the biggest fight of his life, against the most prominent opponent he will ever face, himself.

The setting begins with the alarm clock going off at four o'clock in the morning. How many people are willing to get up at 4:00 a.m. to become excellent? Once Rocky turns off the alarm, he turns on the transistor radio, and a Philadelphia radio station is playing in the background. If you listen carefully, the weather report on the radio states that the high temperature will be below freezing. How many people are going to pursue excellence in the cold, frigid winter?

Rocky then stumbles to the refrigerator and cracks those five raw eggs into a cup and chugs them down. How many people would refuse to hunt excellence if they didn't have the right food to eat? After breakfast, he puts on his tattered, worn cotton sweatsuit and his black high-top basketball shoes. He puts a towel around his neck and a cap on his head. How many people would refuse to follow the behavior necessary for excellence because they didn't have the right equipment? Who would wait to pursue their dreams until they had the latest moisture-wicking clothing or the top of the line running shoes or cross-trainers?

Rocky then heads down the steps from his apartment and out into the cold, crisp morning air and does some basic stretching outside of his building. How many people would find the excuse of not pursuing excellence because they didn't have their personal trainer or their running buddy available to encourage them along the way?

And then Rocky begins to jog down the dark empty streets of Philadelphia until he finds himself at the base of the seventy-two steps that lead to the fountain in front of the Philadelphia Museum of Art. But he's hurting; he has a pain in his side. How many people would have said, "I have this twinge in my side? I'm done for today. I don't like being in pain. I'll chase excellence when I'm not hurting as much."

Finally, Rocky struggles to the top of the museum steps, and he is doubled over in agony. He is alone, in the dark and the cold. And Rocky realizes that if he is going to be able to go toe to toe with the heavyweight champion of the world, he will have to do the same training regimen tomorrow, only better.

How many people would have given up on their pursuit of excellence when they were at their lowest? How many souls would have thrown any potential opportunity to achieve excellence out the window because they were tired, lonely, hungry, or hurting?

The boxer, Mike Tyson, once said, "Everyone has a plan until they get hit in the mouth." During my cancer journey, I came to a point where I was tagged in the mouth, and things seemed extremely bleak. I was at my lowest. I felt as though I was in the grips of total helplessness and hopelessness. This despair bounded into my life in 2017.

After just completing an almost five-year cycle of the drug Interferon, my melanoma had returned. My oncologist suggested that I start a biological therapy that would do nothing to the cancer but would hopefully cause my immune system to kick in and kill the marauding disease.

I had just finished my fourth and final round of this biologic therapy, which left me exhausted. A week later, I was diagnosed with pseudogout when my right knee swelled to the size of a cantaloupe. The fluid in my knee contained calcium crystals, acting like miniature knives stabbing the inside of the joint every time I moved. That was followed a few weeks later by a reaction to the biologic medication that gave me a blood clot in my lung and fluid around the sac of my heart. I woke up in the middle of the night with chest pains and difficulty breathing. I thought I was having a heart attack, and my wife rushed me to the emergency room.

Lying in the emergency room, I remember feeling so depleted mentally and physically that I looked at my wife, with tears running down my cheeks, and begged her to let me die. I just wanted out of my body that seemed to be attacking me continually.

At that time, I remembered reading an article about the owner of a professional sports team who paid a Navy SEAL to come and live with his family for a month and teach them to use their minds to do more than their bodies ever thought they could.

Part of this training was the 40% Rule. This rule says that if your mind or body is telling you that you are through and can't go on, you are only at 40% of your maximum ability, and you still have 60% left in reserve.

I recall lying in the ER and having doctors, nurses, and technicians performing all types of tests. As horrible as I felt, I remember blocking out everything that was going on around me and telling myself that I had so much more left to give. Even though my body was declaring I was at the end of my rope and just wanted to let go, I forced my mind to inform my body to tie a knot at the end of that rope and simply hang on.

Realizing I had another 60% left in reserve literally saved my life by forcing my mind and body to draw on those reserves that I still possessed.

We all have those stockpiles waiting to be used if we ever get to the point we think we are finished. I would encourage you to draw on those reserves if you ever feel like you can't or don't want to continue toward your purpose. I can speak from personal experience that even when you don't think you can move forward, you have so much more left to give yourself.

I have learned that excellence comes to us when we continue to advance in the face of overwhelming adversity; when we don't think we have anything left in our tanks. Excellence appears when we can strive for our dreams at the lowest points in our lives. We can finally define *our* excellence when we can force our minds and bodies to serve us long after they are gone and be able to hold on when there is nothing left within us except the desire that says to them: "Hold on!"

PRINCIPLE # 1 – ENJOY YOUR LIFE

Don't find a job, or a position, or even a career. Find your passions or your purpose or your why. But to live your purpose, your purpose will need to be bigger than your pain.

———————

MARK TWAIN SAID THAT THE TWO MOST IMPORTANT DAYS OF OUR LIVES are the day we are born and the day we figure out why.

Some time ago, a player I coached when I was a high school girls basketball coach in Houston, Texas, moved to Colorado.

During a text message exchange, I told her I was glad she was living close to my family because it allowed me to watch her find and live her purpose. She responded by asking me what I thought her purpose was. I shared with her the quote from Mark Twain and explained that I didn't know what her purpose was, only she could determine that. I went on to tell her that the only way she would find her purpose was to be open to it and search for it with her heart. I explained that some people take ten or twenty years to find their calling while others know instantly what they were born to do. But when your "why" presents

I

itself, you will know it. One thing about your purpose is that, once you find it, it will bring you peace.

I explained that finding your purpose involves taking an active role in determining your destiny. Life is not so much about *finding* your purpose as it is *designing* your purpose based on your beliefs. But you can't just sit back and hope your purpose finds you. In creating your purpose, you have to search for it by trying different things. Many of those endeavors may cause you to fail which, believe it or not, can be a blessing in your life. Failure is a decisive factor because it teaches you two things. It shows you what you like and don't like and it teaches you to be resilient. To get off the floor when life knocks you down. It gives you grit.

Unfortunately, I've seen too many people stop searching for their "why" and settle for a life that doesn't inspire them or make them happy. If you aren't excited to get out of bed each morning, you aren't living your purpose. I told her I hoped she would continue to seek her purpose and never stop until she found it. If she did that, she would end up living an uncommon and extraordinary life, on top of being fulfilled as a person.

I also reminded her that Colonel Harland Sanders, the founder of Kentucky Fried Chicken, didn't start the company until after he retired. I don't know if the creation of the company that sells that delicious chicken was the colonel's purpose in life, but I wanted her to realize that sometimes it takes a lifetime of exploring to find the reason God put you in this world.

I believe my calling has always been law enforcement. On my father's side, my grandfather was a Chicago police officer from the 1920s until the 1950s. As such, he was a police officer in Chicago during Prohibition and at the height of the crime syndicates who terrorized the city.

On April 24, 1932, my grandfather was a detective assigned to the Chicago Police detective bureau. He was escorting a suspected bank robber and murderer back to his cell after an interview in the captain's office, when the suspect seized my grandfather's .38 service revolver from his shoulder holster, causing an intense struggle for the deadly weapon. Although other officers saw the move by this killer, and immediately came to my grandfather's aid, the suspect managed to discharge a single round from the weapon, wounding my grandfather in the right ankle, before he was disarmed and subdued.

My father was just an infant when his dad was shot in the line of duty. However, the event had a traumatic impact on his life. As an adult, he had the vivid memories told to him by his mother of the Chicago Police command staff showing up at their apartment and escorting the family to the hospital to await the outcome of my grandfather's surgery.

Because of this childhood trauma, my father was adamantly opposed to me ever pursuing a career in law enforcement. Even though being a policeman was my passion, my father did everything he could to block my entry into the criminal justice field.

I had a profound interest in being a member of the Secret Service after I graduated from college. While my dad wasn't extremely overt about blocking my passion, he went about it more surreptitiously.

Dad knew the Special Agent in Charge (SAC) of the Columbus, Ohio, office of the Secret Service. As a way of pacifying my interest in joining the Service, he arranged for me to interview with the SAC.

I was excited as I drove to the interview at the Federal Building in downtown Columbus. Since my Dad knew the SAC, I thought that I had a better than average opportunity to be selected for the Secret Service.

The agent was exceedingly polite as he greeted me and ushered me into his office. It was a humid summer day in Columbus, and I recall baking in a three-piece suit as I spent two hours being grilled about my background and interests while the agent sat at his desk in a short-sleeved shirt with the fan blowing in his direction. By the time the interview concluded, I had perspired so much that my shirt, vest, and suit jacket were saturated.

I didn't learn until years later that the entire interview was nothing more than a ruse to make it seem like I had been considered for a position as an agent only to be turned down because I didn't have a master's degree.

Although my dad had hoped this rejection would blunt my desire for a law enforcement career, it did just the opposite. Unfortunately for me, my Dad was personal friends with the Columbus police chief and the Franklin County sheriff. Since I persisted in my desire to find a job in criminal justice, my dad arranged for the sheriff to swear me in as a special deputy. While I was excited to carry the badge, the title was only ceremonial and didn't come with any training or responsibility. Nevertheless, it kept my dream alive of one day becoming a lawman.

Since I didn't feel I could go against my father's wishes at that time, I took a job as a field marketing trainee in the marketing department at the corporate offices of Wendy's International, the fast-food chain, in Dublin, Ohio.

While most of the people I worked with were exceptional, I didn't have a passion for analyzing statistics that determined who ate what, where, when, why, and with whom. I wasn't excited to get up in the morning and go to work. I knew I hadn't found my passion and was anxious that I appeared to be just marking time.

The most beneficial part of working for Wendy's was the fact that my father was the senior vice president for real estate, engineering, and construction and worked in the same building as I did. This relationship was crucial because shortly after I started working at Wendy's, my father was diagnosed with end-stage breast cancer.

I say it was beneficial because most weekdays, my day would start with me getting up and going into my parents' bedroom to empty my father's urinal. I would then shower, get dressed, eat breakfast, and drive to work. Around lunchtime, I would drive home, help my mother get my father dressed, assist him down the stairs, and into my car. We would then make the ten-minute drive back to the office, park my car in front of the building, and escort my father to his office on the second floor. Once I had Dad safely situated at work, I'd go back to my car, and move it to the employee lot and return to my job.

When quitting time rolled around, I'd get back in my car and drive around to the front of the building. I'd then go to Dad's office and help him into my vehicle for the short drive home. Once we were home, I'd assist him into the house and back to his bedroom where Mom and I would help him undress and put him to bed for the evening.

This weekday ritual may seem like a mundane set of activities, but I believe it played a central role in my father living for another three and a half years after his terminal diagnosis. At work, Dad had a purpose. His passion was real estate. Before taking the position at Wendy's, he spent most of his career working his way up to the national director of real estate for McDonald's Corporation. He loved finding exceptional locations for new restaurants and negotiating the deal to secure the property. One of his most significant accomplishments was being part of the team that instituted the first fast-food restaurant on a college campus when McDonald's and The Ohio State University agreed to locate a restaurant in the student union.

Even though Dad was dying of this horrible disease, his passion for running the real estate department at Wendy's gave him a reason to live.

As I was eventually promoted to a supervisor and moved to the new products marketing department, I knew my time at Wendy's was limited as the bottom was falling out of the fast-food industry. The company was looking to make personnel cuts.

Still having the passion for entering the law enforcement field but not wanting to defy my dying father, my next job was with an eleven hundred bed, 5,000 employee hospital along the banks of the Olentangy River, called Riverside Methodist Hospital.

I was hired as the manager of new programs and charged with running a new concept the chief executive officer had instituted called "Champions of Innovation." In my role, I was responsible for working with individual employees or departments to develop and implement new programs, medical testing, or equipment to aid our patients and contribute to the hospital's bottom line.

During my time at Riverside, two life-altering events occurred, my father died, and my wife Roberta and I were married.

After our marriage, Roberta and I relocated to Santa Barbara, California, as she had taken a job with a boutique financial management company.

One day, we received a catalog of the course offerings at Santa Barbara City College. Normally, I would have pitched the catalog when it arrived in the mail, but for some reason, I decided to peruse the course offerings.

To my surprise, I noticed a class that, once completed, allowed the student to apply to be a reserve police officer with any law enforcement agency in California. The course was offered at night, so it wouldn't infringe on my day job, and was primarily taught by a sergeant from the Santa Barbara Police Department.

At dinner that evening, I asked Roberta what she thought about me taking the course and, if possible, applying to the Santa Barbara Police Department as a reserve officer. She indicated that if it was something that interested me, I should give it a try.

Given that I routinely threw away the Santa Barbara City College catalogs when they arrived in the mail, I have often wondered if it was divine providence that I happened to leaf through that particular catalog. Was there some force that guided me to the course offering for a reserve police officer? I will never know the answer to that question, but I have always believed that you need to be open to finding your purpose and search for it with your heart, even if that purpose happens to show up in the mail.

I never stopped wanting to be a police officer. It was a desire that always burned inside me and still does to this day. I never closed my heart to what I believed my purpose was. If I had, I doubt I would have come across the course offering.

Shortly after my initial text with my former player who moved to Colorado, she followed up and asked me if I had any thoughts on how she could go about finding her purpose. I replied by telling her to answer these five questions. I recommended that she not just provide superficial responses, but spend some time in thought to dive deep for the answers.

1. What makes you the unique person you are? What separates you from your friends and family? What would others say you are the best at doing?
2. What would you define as your passions? What tasks or hobbies make you want to get out of bed every morning and pursue? Is your current job part of the desires you identified? Why or why not?
3. What can you do to make the world a better place? What passions have you identified that you could use to give back to the world with your many blessings?
4. If you could design your ideal life, what would that be? What things would you be doing, and who would be part of that perfect life?
5. What are you willing to sacrifice to live your uncommon and extraordinary life?

Too many people want to find a job, or a position, or a career. While there is nothing wrong with wanting to be employed, how dedicated are you going to be working at something that doesn't inspire and motivate you?

A few years ago, my nephew, Ryan, asked me about his career path after college. Ryan had recently graduated from the University of Illinois and was a walk-on punter for the Illini football team. One of the things I tried to stress with him was that he should never take a job solely based on the amount of money he would make.

All the job satisfaction surveys I have ever read ranked salary from # 4 to # 8 in terms of importance. Being valued for your ideas, having a flexible schedule to deal with child and family needs, and even benefits always ranked higher than how much money a person made.

Ryan eventually took a sales position in the Chicago area. After a few years of a successful sales career, he was offered a job where he could be a recruiter at the Catholic high school where he graduated, Marist. The upside of the recruiter job was that he felt he could have a positive impact on the lives of young people. The downside was that he would be taking a substantial pay cut.

Ryan was at an impasse in his professional career. He had to decide between the importance of a lucrative sales job selling a product he wasn't passionate about or touching and shaping young people's minds and hearts. After some careful consideration, he chose to follow his passion and live a life of service to others by becoming a recruiter at Marist High School.

One of Ryan's gifts is his ability to connect with others. That is what made him successful in sales. It is also what made him effective as a recruiter. Ryan's talent for bonding with others made him passionate about going to work. His skill in developing relationships made room for him to work in sales or to recruit. Ryan used his gifts to *create* his purpose.

On March 20, 1925, Frederick Lewis Donaldson gave a sermon in Westminster Abbey in London, where he listed the Seven Social Sins. The first one he recorded was: Wealth Without Work. That was followed by Pleasure Without Conscience, Knowledge Without Character, Commerce Without Morality, Science Without Humanity, Worship Without Sacrifice, and Politics Without Principle.

Donaldson drew a direct comparison between the importance of work and morality when it came to business or money. Without hard work conducted in an honorable manner, the acquisition of wealth has little meaning and, in many cases, can be sinful.

The simple advice I gave Ryan several years ago is one of those recommendations that are universal. You will be happier (and in many cases, work harder) if you seek a position where you can find and live your purpose.

Unfortunately, many people worry and obsess about finding and living their purpose. You will never obtain your passion if you always worry about it. Finding your purpose is not hard. Finding your purpose is not easy. Finding your purpose is about stilling yourself and listening for the direction you should move. Finding your purpose is not about doing things for the sake of doing them; it is about doing something that fosters and nurtures your unique gifts.

For me to live my dream, the purpose of my life had to be bigger than the obstacles that were put in my path to prevent me from finding and living my uncommon and extraordinary life.

We all need employment to meet our basic needs. But once those fundamental needs are met, I recommend you take the time to determine what your reason on this planet is. Ask yourself, "Why was I born?" Maybe take that a step further and raise the question, "Why was I born at this time?" There is a reason you were born, and that reason involves finding and living your uncommon and extraordinary life.

Once you have determined that purpose, your next question should be, "What do I need to do to realize the 'why' in my life?" Do you need additional training or education? Do you need a mentor to help guide you along the right path? Are there current habits that are separating you from your uncommon and extraordinary life?

When I was in grade school in Columbus, Ohio, my best friend was a Japanese boy named Ken. Ken and I spent a great deal of time at each other's house. His parents were very traditional when it came to Japanese customs and practices.

I admired the way Ken's parents did everything with simplicity, perfection, and attention to detail. No task was too mundane to give it the time and attention it deserved.

I was always self-conscious when I ate at Ken's house because his parents were precise and detail-orientated when preparing and serving the meal. To them, it wasn't just dinner, it was a work of art that they had done their best to make perfect. My American way of eating was so harsh and barbaric. I felt like I was just bellying up to the table and shoveling in the food. Ken's parents savored every bite and took their time serving their guests, so the food was served without compromise. Not even the smallest detail was overlooked, from the napkins' meticulous placement to the serving dishes' exact location. Everything had purpose and importance.

I was once asked if I thought some people might have more than one purpose. After thinking about it, my response was, "Yes." I believe there are times when our goal might be to put our life on hold and care for others. There may be other times when we are self-directed to focus on our specific needs or goals. Sometimes your purpose concludes. That is the time to find your purpose 2.0.

As much as I have considered finding and living your uncommon and extraordinary life, I am convinced that the overriding narrative in your life has to be that you approach the "why" of your existence with an open heart. If you close yourself off to any of the circumstances or opportunities present in your life each day, you may effectively limit your happiness and fulfillment as your meaning in life brushes past you like a breeze in the night.

I can't imagine missing out on why I was put here by our God because I was so focused in a singular area and wasn't able to see the wonder and grandeur that was right in front of me.

It's been suggested that, for many people, there isn't enough time to find and live your purpose. My response is always the same. God has put you on this earth for a reason. Your job is to search out and find that intention, no matter how difficult or frightening it may be. And if you are willing to invest the time to seek and live your purpose, God will always ensure there is enough time for you to make that happen. I would hate to die before I accomplished the reason I was born.

The problem lies in our *quick service* culture that wants immediate gratification and success at everything we attempt. We want our "rewards" immediately and aren't willing to put in the time to get a little better every day. We want our compensations based on our time. This is why so many people are miserable with their daily lives. They don't understand that we are all operating on God's time. The sooner we realize that God's time is most likely not our time, we will have the peace in our hearts to recognize that everything we do or are exposed to may lead us to the ultimate love that God has put in our hearts, the satisfaction that we have found our purpose and lived our uncommon and extraordinary lives.

PRINCIPLE # 2: MOST PEOPLE THINK WITH THEIR FEARS AND INSECURITIES INSTEAD OF USING THEIR MINDS

Learn to think critically. Control your mind, or it will control you. Your mind knows your fears; it knows your insecurities, identifies your vulnerabilities, and uses them against you.

RALPH WALDO EMERSON ONCE SAID, "ALWAYS DO WHAT YOU ARE afraid to do." But how many of us do that?

Up until I was fourteen or fifteen, I was loaded with self-confidence, especially on the basketball court. During my eighth-grade basketball season at St. Anthony Parish in Columbus, Ohio, our team won the Boys' Basketball of America State and National Championships. During my freshman year of high school at St. Charles Preparatory in Columbus, Ohio, I split my time between the junior varsity and varsity basketball teams. The junior varsity team went a perfect 18-0, won the Columbus Catholic League title, and I led the team in scoring and rebounding with twelve points and ten rebounds, respectively. The varsity team went 15-7, won the Columbus Catholic League, won the Class AA Sectional title, and reached the district finals.

The summer between my freshman and sophomore year in high school, our family moved from Columbus, Ohio, to Chicago, Illinois. I went from attending St Charles High School with a student body of 500 to Marist High School with a student body of almost 2,000.

I also tore a cartilage in my right knee during a pick-up basketball game and had surgery to remove it. After the surgery, the wound became infected, and I developed a high fever. It was speculated that because of this infection, scar tissue didn't grow in the area between the bones where the cartilage was removed.

As a result, when I went back playing basketball, I experienced the discomfort of bone-on-bone pain. Because of the trauma to the bones, the joint continually swelled, and it got to the point where I had fluid drained from my knee every few weeks.

My surgeon was puzzled as to why my knee wouldn't heal, which resulted in a second exploratory operation the summer between my sophomore and junior year in high school. This was a time before MRI and CAT scan imagery was available.

The outcome of that second surgery was the removal of twenty-five pieces of my bone that had chipped away, some of them as large as pieces of rice. After surgery, I was placed in a cast from my hip to my ankle and told my basketball playing days were over, and I might not walk normally again.

I was in that cast for the entire summer with nothing to do but wait and wonder what the future held for me.

At this point in my life, I was just fifteen years old. The only success I had experienced so far had been on the basketball court. Because of my drive to succeed and my passion for the game, I refused to accept the doctor's prediction and knew I had to at least try to play again.

When the cast was removed, shortly before school started, I was faced with a thigh muscle that had significantly atrophied from months of inactivity.

After my surgeon examined the wound, he handed me a piece of paper with exercises described in words and drawings for my rehab at home. He shook my hand, wished me luck, and turned to leave the exam room. As he was going, I began peppering him with all kinds of questions: "How many repetitions of each exercise should I do?" "How often should I do each exercise?" "What happens if the knee swells again?"

His reply was intended to address my knee rehabilitation specifically but was profound in its far-reaching impact on my life. Unfortunately, it took until I was much older before I fully understood what he was trying to explain.

He told me to listen to my body for guidance regarding the number of repetitions I should perform and how often I should do each exercise. If there was no pain, he told me to exercise more frequently and perform additional repetitions. If the knee hurt or swelled when I trained, I should use less weight and do fewer repetitions. "Your body will tell you what to do," he said. "Listen to it."

So that's what I did. I went home and began doing the exercises three times a day, every day. As my leg grew stronger, I increased the amount of weight I was using and the number of repetitions I was performing. Once I was able to build back my quadricep, eventually, I was ready to start walking. Walking progressed to jogging, and jogging ultimately led to running.

But the one constant in all this was my mind. Every day I had to battle my mind for supremacy because my brain allowed doubt, fear, and anxiety to creep into my thoughts. My mind was questioning if I would ever make it back on the basketball court. It filled me with uncertainty and insecurity. My mind knew my fears, it recognized my vulnerabilities, and it knew my weaknesses. And it used them against me at every opportunity.

As a result, I began thinking with my fears and insecurities instead of using my mind. Why did I imagine that I would never be able to play basketball again when I hadn't even tried? It was because my mind was attacking me and using my fears and insecurities against me. Even when I made it back on the basketball court, there was always a little voice in the back of my head that was continually reminding me that I wasn't that good anymore, and I didn't belong on the court with the best players in the Chicagoland area. I always felt like I was a step slower, or my skills had deteriorated just like my thigh muscle did from all those months of inactivity.

Although I had three knee surgeries in high school, I was still being recruited by NCAA Division I schools. Several universities in the MidAmerican Conference and the Southern Conference were recruiting me. "Coach K" sat on my parents' couch in Oak Lawn, Illinois, on a bitterly cold February night and offered me the opportunity to play for him at West Point. I even had the head coach for the University of Kentucky call me one Saturday morning to gauge my interest in Kentucky. This call was significant because Kentucky was the defending national champion.

To these coaches and universities, I was still a viable college prospect. But in my mind, I was damaged goods. My thoughts told me that my two years of knee surgeries and rehab had reduced me from an elite athlete to an average player, and I believed the garbage my brain was spewing forth.

Critical thinking should have told me that because top colleges were still recruiting me, my talents and abilities were still at an elite level. Again, I couldn't shake the doubt and uncertainty that I didn't belong on that level.

This negative thinking plagued me through my senior year in high school and my time playing in college. Despite my knee problems, I would have been a much better college player if I had been able to get out of my head and enjoy playing the game I loved.

I recall an incident when I was coaching about the paralyzing power of fear.

When I was coaching the girls' varsity basketball team in Houston, I motioned to the bench for one of the players, Sarah, to go into the game. I then turned around and began observing what was happening on the court. When I turned back around, Sarah was still sitting on the bench. I walked down to where she was seated and told her I wanted her to go into the game for Mikela. She shook her head in agreement as she took off her warm-up top. Again, I turned my attention toward the action on the court as I walked toward the scorer's table. When I turned around, Sarah was still sitting on the bench.

I had never experienced a player who didn't want to go into the game. Finally, I called her to where I was standing and told her to check-in at the scorer's table and replace Mikela. Tears slowly welled up in her eyes as she told me she didn't want to go into the game. When I asked her why she didn't want to play, she told me she was afraid of making a mistake and was afraid her friends would laugh at her.

With my hands on her shoulders, and with the game being played just feet from us, I looked her in the eye and explained that her teammates were counting on her to do her best. I told her I knew she was going to make mistakes, but I needed her in the game. I told her there were no "uniform wearers" on this team. We had a responsibility to each other to do our best every day.

After some additional cajoling and persuading, Sarah finally went into the game and did the best she could. But I couldn't get over how someone who worked hard every day in practice, didn't want to play in the game. Her fear of making a mistake was so overwhelming that it paralyzed her from getting off the bench and helping her teammates.

We don't like to live in an uncomfortable state, but that is the only place where real growth can occur. As a coach, I continuously reminded my players that they needed to become comfortable with being uncomfortable. As such, I would move players in and out of drills during practice that I knew caused them anxiety. I wanted them to be uneasy. Not because I was trying to get them to fail, but because I wanted them to realize they could succeed at something that made them apprehensive.

The only way we can grow, the only way we can push past our comfort zones is to do what we find unpleasant and undesirable. It's in those painful, challenging, and sometimes embarrassing moments that real growth can occur. And when improvement happens, that's when the common can become uncommon, and the ordinary can become extraordinary.

In 1976, the United States gold-medal-winning Olympic swimmer Shirley Babashoff had one of the greatest quotes I have ever heard. It went like this: "Winners think about what they want to happen, losers think about what they don't want to happen."

Winners can override their brains and concentrate on the things they want to occur. Losers focus on the negative aspects of competition and cannot visualize the positive qualities of pursuing a goal or a dream.

This destructive thinking even spilled over into my life outside basketball at The Citadel. Being somewhat immature, nostalgic, and 1,000 miles from home, I began to doubt that I would make it through the rigorous military training, the demanding academics and being part of a major college basketball team.

At one point early in my freshman year, I had convinced myself that I wouldn't be successful at The Citadel. I decided to give up a full scholarship and quit. I had never quit anything in my life, but I was so focused on all the negative thoughts my mind was putting forth that I was going to give up a free college education!

As I walked over to McAlister Fieldhouse to tell the coaches I was leaving; I decided to stop by Mark Clark Hall and see if I had any mail. As luck would have it, I had a letter from my father. I took the note to the Fieldhouse and climbed the steps to the very top of the arena where no one would see me, and opened it.

I had never received a letter from my father. Still, in seven handwritten pages, my Dad told me how proud he was of me for overcoming my knee issues and getting a scholarship to play basketball at the college level. He said that he had expected more of me than he did of my brothers because I had always delivered when things were difficult. He went on to tell me my priorities were out of balance. I was so focused on myself that I was missing the big picture of everything and everyone that was going on around me. Finally, he told me that he was confident I could not only be successful at The Citadel but also excel. But success or failure was entirely dependent on me, my attitude, and the effort I was willing to put forward to succeed.

By the time I finished reading the letter, I was in tears. How could I possibly quit after what my father had written? There was absolutely no way I could go back to Chicago with my shaved head and be labeled a quitter. This letter was a defining moment in my life. If I had given up, it would have adversely changed my life direction forever. So, I folded the letter in half, wiped my eyes with the handkerchief that every Citadel cadet was required to carry in his back pocket, and headed back to the barracks determined to give it my best effort in the hope that I wouldn't let my father down.

While I still had the nagging feeling that I didn't belong, I managed to earn a varsity letter all four years I was on The Citadel basketball team and was a co-captain of the team my senior year. I also graduated, although barely, with a business administration degree in four years.

I still have my father's letter safely tucked away in a safe deposit box. I've often wondered about the coincidence of receiving his correspondence at the precise moment it was needed. If there hadn't been a letter in my mailbox on my way to the Fieldhouse that day, would I have quit and never become a member of The Citadel's "Long Gray Line?"

I tend to believe that divine intervention asserts itself when we stray off the path that will lead us to our uncommon and extraordinary purpose. But the choice to continue down our current route or have a course correction to get back on our intended road is entirely up to us. While I believe life tries to help you when you wander off your planned course, the decision on which direction to go is ultimately up to you. We have free will to decide we want to be common and ordinary, or we want to take the road less traveled and strive to become uncommon and extraordinary.

Years ago, I saw a YouTube video that detailed a story about a glass of water. The story went like this:

A psychologist was teaching a stress management class to an audience. She raised a glass of water and asked everyone, "How heavy is this glass of water?" Expecting another "Half-full/half-empty" question, the onlookers gave various answers…15 oz! 22oz? 14oz. "Well," she said, "the absolute weight of the glass of water doesn't really matter. It depends on how long you hold it. A minute won't be a problem. After an hour, you might feel a dull ache, and if you hold it for a day, your arm might feel paralyzed. But, the weight of the water never changed. The longer you hold it, the heavier it feels." The stress and worries of our lives are just like the glass of water. If you consider them once in a while, nothing happens. If you dwell on them, you start to hurt, and if you think about them all the time, you feel paralyzed and helpless. Learn to put the glass of water down and focus on the positive things you have in your life.

Most people will never get to where they want because they won't stop whining and complaining about where they are. If you are going to lead an uncommon and extraordinary life, the only way to make that happen is to embrace the uncomfortable and continue to do the things you don't like, and you don't want to do. To be successful, your purpose has to be bigger than your pain.

The concept of controlling your fears and insecurities is something most people have a difficult time understanding. I've found the following model makes it easier to understand. If you pick up a ten-pound weight and do ten arm curls, but don't find the movement painful, your muscles will never grow. However, if you take that same ten-pound weight and do arm curls until you exhaust your muscle and can't do another repetition, you are stressing that muscle, and as a result, it will grow and get stronger. That same tactic works with your mind. If you stress or push your mind by doing uncomfortable things, it will grow, develop, and you will become a stronger and more resolute individual.

It wasn't until my cancer diagnosis that I truly began to harden my mind so that I could make decisions that were in my best interest based on facts instead of the fears and vulnerabilities the disease or treatments were causing me.

Having knee surgery as a high school student was frightening, but being diagnosed with a life-threatening illness like cancer was devastating.

I was fifty-one years old when I had a callus break open on the bottom of my foot. Since I was a high school basketball coach and on my feet for many hours a day because of practices and games, I didn't give the wound much attention. After a few weeks of the injury not healing, I eventually went to a doctor who tried various techniques to get the wound to close. Finally, he decided I had a cyst that prevented the healing process and removed it in a simple surgical procedure in his office. After the surgery, he showed me the transparent gelatin sac with a white fatty substance inside. He reassured me that everything looked normal but that he would send the cyst to pathology to confirm the diagnosis.

Two weeks later, I received a call from my doctor dropping the news that my benign cyst was, in fact, a rare and deadly form of melanoma that only about 6,500 people in the United States are diagnosed with each year.

This unwelcome news was the beginning of a tremendous amount of mental and physical suffering that my family and I experienced. While I make no claims to have the market cornered on suffering, I learned that suffering is one of life's greatest teachers.

I had two surgeries to remove the tumor and all the lymph nodes in my groin and had a skin graft to close the wound on the bottom of my foot where the melanoma was removed. When I healed from the surgeries, I was placed on a weekly injection of the drug Interferon to keep the disease from returning.

While I realize that people react differently to Interferon, for me, the drug was a nasty, horrible, and debilitating experience. I took those weekly injections for almost five years before the medication became so toxic to my body that I ended up in the intensive care unit with a fever of 108 degrees.

I lost fifty pounds during my Interferon therapy. I was always nauseous, fatigued, and chilled, my ability to taste food diminished, and my body continually ached. This misery went on for over 1,660 days.

One thing I learned during all my pain and suffering is that you have two choices. You can succumb to the debilitating discomfort and misery, or you can learn to embrace it and use it to make you a stronger and more determined human being. I chose the latter.

Please understand that there were days I felt so poorly and was in so much agony that I prayed to die. I just wanted out of this life. Each day was a struggle to use my mind to override the apathy and distress my body was feeling.

I was no better at dealing with pain and discomfort. But every day, I found a way to survive, with the knowledge that I would need to do it again the following morning.

I understand what it is like to fight for your life. And the one thing I have learned is that as long as you don't quit, as long as you don't allow your mind to be hijacked, you can never be defeated.

PRINCIPLE #3 – YOU WERE BORN TO LIVE AN UNCOMMON AND EXTRAORDINARY LIFE

But to lead this type of life, you need to do the things that scare you, and you don't want to do. That is the only way you will grow. You need to keep moving forward and remind yourself that as long as you don't quit, you can never be defeated.

COMMON AND ORDINARY PEOPLE DO NOTHING WITH THEIR LIVES, BUT uncommon and extraordinary people can accomplish anything.

But what does an uncommon and extraordinary life entail? Being uncommon and extraordinary has absolutely nothing to do with what type of job we work, how much money we make, what kind of car we drive, where we live, etc. We are not all born with the same gifts and talents. But we all can become the best person we are capable of becoming.

John Wooden, the famed UCLA basketball coach, even used this concept when he described success. Coach Wooden defined success as "peace of mind which is a direct result of self-satisfaction in knowing you did your best to become the best you are capable of becoming."

During the numerous years of battling cancer, I've had plenty of time to think about my death. After I die, I can't imagine standing in the presence of our Creator and being unable to account for the gifts and talents I was born with and that I didn't use to make the world a better place.

Throughout my life, I have, unfortunately, seen many people die. I've watched my father and grandmother pass away. I've seen victims of homicide, and I've been in the hospital room as my good friend Kathy took her last breath, after years of fighting leukemia. It has been my experience that the people who die what we would call *peaceful deaths* are those who utilized their time on earth to find and live their purpose. On the other hand, many of the people I observed go kicking and screaming from this world, who were begging for another day, or another month, or just one more year, were people who never did anything with their lives. They never saw the urgency of living their uncommon and extraordinary purpose.

These people never took a chance on their dreams. They never took the time to figure out who they were, why they were here, and what they were supposed to do with their lives.

Years ago, I heard a Native American Blackfoot proverb that has always stuck with me. It goes like this, "When you were born, you cried, and the world rejoiced. Live your life in such a way so that when you die, the world cries and you rejoice."

The only way to find your purpose is to search it out. To try things that make you uncomfortable, to fight against the status quo, and experience something that scares you.

But living an uncommon and extraordinary life doesn't mean you have to be famous or influential. I would argue the peace, simplicity, and serenity of your life provides you the fostering backdrop to lead your uncommon and extraordinary life.

The great Native American Shawnee chief Tecumseh wrote an interesting poem about the virtues necessary to lead a meaningful and purposeful life. The poem goes like this:

"So, live your life that the fear of death can never enter your heart.

Trouble no one about their religion; respect others in their views and demand they respect yours.

Love your life, perfect your life, beautify all things in your life. Seek to make your life long and its purpose in service to your people. Prepare a noble death song for the day when you go over the great divide.

Always give a word or a sign of salute when meeting or passing a friend, even a stranger, when in a lonely place.

Show respect to all people and grovel to none.

When you arise in the morning, give thanks for the food and the joy of living. If you see no reason to give thanks, the fault lies only in yourself.

Abuse no one and no thing, for abuse turns wise ones to fools and robs the spirit of its vision.

When it comes your time to die, be unlike those whose hearts are filled with the fear of death, so that when their time comes, they weep and pray for more time to live their lives over again in a different way. Sing your death song and die like a hero going home."

Too many people consider an uncommon or extraordinary life to be tied to money, influence, or power. I believe Tecumseh's poem details the unpretentiousness of living an exceptional life, but it doesn't say a word about wealth, power, or prestige.

My wife, Roberta, had a friend and mentor who was very successful on Wall Street. I'll call him Garret. Garret was a powerful individual in a prominent New York financial firm. Garret had a gorgeous house in Greenwich, Connecticut, an apartment in Manhattan, and more money than most of us could ever imagine. He also had a lovely wife and three healthy children.

Garret was on the board of several companies and a prestigious business school. By all outward appearances, you would say that Garret was leading an uncommon and extraordinary life.

However, Garret's pursuit of wealth and power caused his marriage to dissolve, and the relationship with his children deteriorated. Eventually, he and his wife divorced, and his children rarely spoke with him, unless they were looking for a handout.

Roberta stayed in touch with Garret during his trials and even when his financial wealth was impacted in the market crash of 2008. Garret seemed to rebound from the economic crisis and dated some high-profile women in the New York area until eventually marrying an artist and purchasing another house in Connecticut.

Even though Garret appeared to recover from his personal and monetary calamities, several years ago he took his own life. I found it interesting to listen to how his friends reacted to this tragedy on social media. Many of them couldn't understand how a person who seemingly had everything he wanted, would decide that his life was worthless and die by his own hand.

I've met a lot of Garrets in my life. Most of them are people who seemed to have the world by the tail. People who have money and influence and power. People who, by all accounts of our materialistic society, would be deemed to be "successful." But of all those people I've met, I wouldn't say any of them lived an uncommon or extraordinary life. Maybe they were flourishing, but none of them appeared content, happy, or at peace.

I don't understand these people nor have I walked in their shoes, but my sense tells me the very "powerful" people have a difficult time growing up or maturing. By that, I mean they were unable to find their uncommon and extraordinary purpose because they never grew out of the selfish phase most young people experience.

When I graduated from The Citadel in 1982, with my newly obtained business administration degree, I was all set to make my mark on the world. I was the first person in my family to graduate from college, and I was positive that I knew what was in my best interest. I wanted to do what I wanted when I wanted and how I wanted. I was the king of my castle, and nobody was going to tell me how to live my life.

Many young people, including myself, think that because we have a college degree, diploma, or skill, we understand life. We are the arbitrator of our existence, and nobody can tell us what to do. We know what we want and what is best for us, and we aren't about to listen to someone who has an opinion or thought that differs from our way of thinking. Our reality is focused inward, and in many instances, we aren't open to finding our purpose and leading our uncommon and extraordinary life. We are selfish and self-serving.

But as we age, grow, and mature, we start to focus our energy outside of ourselves and realize we aren't in control of our individuality despite what we might think. Many times, this maturation occurs because we add others into our lives. We take on a spouse and possibly children. Some of us take on the responsibility of an aging parent. As we rise in our careers, we come to understand the immense responsibility we have for the employees who count on us for their daily existence.

As we grow, we realize that our decisions have a much broader reach than just *our* lives. We may be the single stone that enters the pond, but we are accountable for all the ripples that stone creates. Our actions affect all those around us, and our life changes from being "me" focused to being "we" focused.

I'd like to share the story of King Alexander III of Macedon, otherwise known as Alexander the Great, and his final three wishes, which I think illustrates the change from "me" to "we" that allows us to live our uncommon and extraordinary lives.

As Alexander the Great lay dying, he summoned his counselors and asked them to carry out his final three wishes. His first wish was that only his physicians carry his coffin to his grave. His second wish was that when his coffin was on the way to his burial plot, that the path leading to the cemetery be strewn with gold, silver, and precious stones. His final wish was that both of his hands be left hanging out of his coffin.

When one of his counselors asked why Alexander had made such strange wishes, he responded, "I would like the world to know what I have learned. I want my physicians to carry my coffin to show people that no doctor can cure anybody. They are powerless to save a person from the grip of death. People shouldn't take life for granted and should be responsible for their health and vitality."

Regarding his second wish, he said, "I want people to understand that not an ounce of my gold will be coming with me to the next life. I spent my entire existence centered on greed and power but can take none of my wealth beyond the grave. Let people realize it is sheer stupidity to chase fortune."

Concerning his hands hanging out of his coffin, he replied, "I want people to see my hands and understand I came into this world empty-handed, and I now leave it in the same manner."

The story of Alexander the Great illustrates what is truly important in life. There is a reason it is called the *practice* of medicine. The noted theologian and physician, Albert Schweitzer, is reported to have said, "The doctor of the future will be oneself." Our bodies are amazing machines. Doctors can help guide us toward well-being, but they don't cure anything. They merely assist the body in healing itself.

Alexander knew that wealth, power, and prestige were fleeting qualities. No matter how prosperous or influential you may be, you won't be able to take any of that money or importance beyond the grave. Regardless of your social status, you will eventually occupy the same small plot of dirt that the pauper does who is buried beside you.

Finally, we come into this world with the breath in our lungs, the thoughts in our minds, and the love in our hearts. Nobody is born with a silver spoon in their hands, and we depart this life more or less the same way we entered it.

Alexander knew this and wanted to impart his wisdom to those he left behind. He wanted his descendants to realize that life is finite, and nothing you have on earth will translate to the next life, except love. He understood that life was meant to be lived and not merely observed. Furthermore, Alexander wanted his subjects to appreciate that life is short, and people shouldn't procrastinate finding and living their uncommon and extraordinary purpose.

We all have a reason as to why we were born. There is no one else, nor will there ever be anyone else, with the unique gifts and talents we possess. Our value comes from who we are, not from what we do. Our spiritual identity cannot be stripped away by anything mortal. We are distinctive from every other human being who ever existed. Our God, the Creator of the Universe, has designed us for a unique purpose. He has freely gifted us with His talents and abilities. No strings attached. Our identity comes from being formed in the unique image and likeness of our God. That inimitability comes from an absolute and incomparable love from our Father.

In 1 Peter 4:10-11, it states:

"God has given each of you a gift from his great variety of spiritual gifts. Use them well to serve one another. Do you have the gift of speaking? Then speak as though God himself were speaking through you. Do you have the gift of helping others? Do it with the strength and energy God supplies. Then everything you do will bring glory to God through Jesus Christ. All glory and power to him forever and ever. Amen."

I don't understand why people are so hesitant to discern their special gifts and use them to make the world, and the lives of those around them, better. I've often wondered if jealousy, or a desire to have what others possess, could be a reason.

In some sense, we aren't comfortable with our uniqueness; we seem to strive for what others have. I've spoken to many people who believe that if they had this certain quality or possessed that ability, their life would somehow be more fulfilled. This attitude goes back to a lack of maturity and continues to be "me" focused.

At the end of your life, God will not judge you by what others did. He won't compare you to how others performed. He will adjudicate you based on how you used your precious and unique gifts to make His world a better place.

If we could focus on being thankful for what we have instead of longing for what others possess, we would be able to concentrate our attention on the gifts that make us special and use those talents in service to our God, our fellow man, and ourselves. That is how you live an uncommon and extraordinary life.

PRINCIPLE #4 – ALWAYS REMAIN CURIOUS AND ASK QUESTIONS

Never be the smartest person in the room and surround yourself with people who will argue with you.

USUALLY WITH TONGUE IN CHEEK, ROBERTA AND I WATCH THE SUNDAY morning news shows. Over the past ten years, I have become more and more disillusioned with the moderators of these programs (who claim to be hard-hitting journalists dedicated to the "truth") because they refuse to ask their guests what I refer to as "the heart question." This is the critical follow-up question that will box the guest into revealing what he or she believes about an issue or where they stand on a particular topic.

It's the heart question that the television audience wants answered. And it's incredibly frustrating when the host leads the guest right to the edge of the cliff and then lets them off the hook by not asking this critical question.

To be effective at something, you need to have the knowledge and an understanding of how things work. If you want to be great at a particular task, add curiosity to your toolbox. You need to ask "why" a lot and learn better and more efficient ways to perform your tasks or chase your dreams. You need to surround yourself with people who are smarter than you and who are willing to tell you the truth, even if the truth is something you don't want to hear.

When I was a police officer in Cincinnati, Ohio, my first assignment out of the police academy was in District 2. After my field training was completed, I was assigned to the night shift and to Beat One, which included the areas of Evanston and East Walnut Hills. The Cincinnati Police Department regularly runs single officer cars. In some neighborhoods, a two-person car was assigned to take all the "hot runs," like domestic violence, shootings, a person with a gun, drugs, etc. There was a two-person car on Beat One. That car number was 2311.

Over about eight months, it became my goal to be one of the officers assigned to car 2311.

Several months after our field training was complete, the officers who usually ran car 2311 were moved to other assignments. When the opening for another 2311 came available, I approached one of my academy classmates, Kim, and floated the idea of us becoming permanent partners and requesting that responsibility. Kim readily agreed, and we went to see our sergeant to request the assignment. Our boss was at the tail end of his thirty-plus year police career and had forgotten more about policing than Kim and I knew. He was extremely reluctant to partner us up because we didn't have a great deal of experience, but he agreed to allow us to run 2311 from time to time to see how we performed.

One of our first challenges was to move the drug dealers off their neighborhood corners. This encounter proved more difficult than expected. The dealers always had spotters, who were mostly on foot, and when a marked police car came into the area, they would whistle to alert the dealer to hide his stash of drugs. The only problem with this warning method was that being on foot didn't enable the spotters to cover much distance, and at times we were able to sneak past these sentinels and catch the dealer red-handed or at least confiscate their stash of drugs.

To expand the area patrolled by the spotters, they began using bicycles to increase the area they were able to cover. The bikes made it that much more difficult to stop the dealers from peddling their narcotics in the neighborhood.

Just because a law exists on the books, doesn't mean it is one that is enforced. Our first thought on how to deal with these pedal-pushing spotters was to peruse the Ohio Vehicle Code and the Cincinnati Municipal Code as they related to bicycles. We learned that anyone over eighteen years of age was prohibited from riding a bike on the sidewalk. Further, the Municipal Code required a bike to have a working bell, a working headlight if operated at night, and a red reflector on the rear of the bicycle.

Those were the statutes, but were they statutes that would be enforced if we wrote the tickets? Before putting our plan into place, we checked with the City Prosecutor, who told us they would prosecute if we wrote those tickets.

Armed with the Municipal Code statutes, we began stopping all the drug dealers' sentinels and writing them $125 tickets for riding on the sidewalk and not having the required equipment on their bike. In some cases, we would write a spotter $375 in fines during a single stop.

We knew the spotters didn't have the money to pay out these citations, which meant either the dealer would have to shell out the funds for the tickets or the spotter would end up with a warrant for their arrest because they failed to pay the fines or appear in court.

We continued this tactic every night for almost three weeks. We kept the names and dates of birth for every spotter we contacted and would "run" them on our in-car computer to see if they had warrants for nonpayment of the fines or not showing up in court. If they had warrants, we would arrest them, take them to jail and impound their bicycles.

After a month of the dealers having to pay the fines or the spotters being arrested, the spotters eventually stopped using bicycles. We were more easily able to either capture the dealers or their buyers or confiscate their stash of drugs.

Over time, Kim and I improved the neighborhood's quality of life by forcing the dealers to move off the corner to sell their drugs. For our hard work and resourcefulness in solving this issue, we were granted the opportunity to be permanent partners with a designated car number, 2311.

Kim and I loved being police officers and enjoyed the four-plus years that we were permanent partners. We always looked for ways to be better at our job and remained curious about how and why things were happening on our beat. In law enforcement terms, we had Beat Pride. We knew the people and places on our beat. This proved beneficial several times when undercover units or detectives were looking for a particular individual who may have been involved in a crime they were investigating. In many instances, we knew the individual in question just based on their physical description. We also knew where he lived, who he hung out with, where his mother lived, and usually where his baby's mother lived.

Not taking things at face value and finding the time to learn about things that puzzle you or you don't understand will help you live your uncommon and extraordinary life.

In 1941, Hans and Margret Rey published the first series of seven children's books about the adventures of an orphaned monkey called *Curious George*.

Curious George was a set of books that our parents read to us as my brothers and I were growing up. The thing I remembered most about George's adventures was how often he was in danger of being captured during his exploits but always managed to elude his abductors.

In reality, many people would have been traumatized by almost being apprehended during their escapades, but not George. George never let fear get in the way of his future quests or exploits. George never allowed the trepidation of the past to color the excitement of the future. The courage and determination *Curious George* always possessed made his series one of the most popular sets of children's books ever written.

Let's face it; we like surrounding ourselves with like-minded people. There is comfort in having friends and acquaintances who act like us, believe what we believe, and always tell us how great we are. While these people may bolster our egos, they provide very little impetus for us to grow. This group values, vindicates, and validates our lifestyle.

While these associates make us feel all warm and fuzzy, they aren't doing anything to help us grow and improve.

I've seen plenty of leaders and people in authority who reward agreement with the boss and punish those who say anything that goes against what the supervisor wants.

How often have you been in a meeting where the boss walks in, sits down, and outlines a problem? He or she then spends some amount of time describing how they believe the problem should be solved. Once they conclude their understanding of the problem and how to fix it, they ask this question: "Does anyone have any other ideas about how we can solve this issue?"

How many people are going to countermand the boss and offer an alternative solution to the problem? It's been my experience that those who are brave enough to comment do nothing more than restate what the boss just said, in a different format. The person in charge explained how the problem should be solved, why would you want to go against those ideas?

A better way to solve complex problems and involve people in determining a solution would be to run a meeting like this.

The boss comes into the meeting and outlines a particular problem or issue. Instead of providing their solution, they ask if anyone has ideas on how the problem can be fixed. In this environment, the boss wants the group to come up with a resolution. Holding back their suggestions provides an opportunity for other perspectives on solving the issue.

All of us must have a posse. To surround ourselves with people who lift us and make us feel validated. I can tell a great deal about a person, their values, and the prospects for their successful future, based on the people who are part of their inner circle.

When I was in my early 30s, I was the customer service manager for a publishing company in California. Before I was hired, the vice president of sales and marketing was responsible for supervising the six employees who made up the customer service staff. Unfortunately, the VP, who lived in another state, would blow into town once a month, and spend a day or two periodically berating these employees for some real or imagined malady she perceived they were guilty of committing.

During the interview process, this negative culture was explained to me, along with the fact that a few of the customer service representatives had expressed interest in transitioning to another area of the company or leaving outright. I got the sense the entire group was about to mutiny.

After I arrived, I met with each of the representatives individually. I wanted to know about their goals, both personally and professionally, where they saw themselves five years from now, and what they saw as the biggest obstacles to having a world-class customer service department.

Overriding everything that was said was the lack of honesty among the group. Everyone I interviewed told me the vice president fostered this attitude. I knew the only way I could salvage this group was to institute a culture where honesty and commitment were promoted and expected.

As such, I began sharing important company information and financials with the group. I either acted on or explained why I was unable to do ideas that had been suggested by the group. There were even times I reversed course on a particular plan after it was pointed out how the suggestion could be implemented.

I knew the culture had shifted during one chilly morning in early December. I had just returned from an early operations meeting when I noticed one of the representatives was not at her desk. When I asked where she was, nobody would look at me. So, I asked again. Finally, one of the younger representatives came over to my desk and told me she had called in sick. Since our policy was that a representative was to call me when they were ill, I asked why she had not contacted me?

I knew it was difficult for this young man, but he mustered up all his courage and told me that she had decided to call in sick and stay home to try to win a radio contest. Typically, he would not have said anything more than she had called in sick. However, he knew her actions weren't honest and believed she wasn't doing what was in the best interest of our group.

I told him I appreciated his honesty, and I knew how difficult it was for him to relate to me the particulars of the story. I asked him to write down as much of the conversation as he could remember verbatim, while I went to talk with the vice president of human resources.

The following morning, when the employee who had called off sick to try to win a radio contest returned to work, she was terminated.

Although the young customer service representative who took the call and relayed the particulars to me felt terrible about his co-worker losing her job, months later, he confided in me that he was glad he came forward and did what was right. He said he would never have gotten involved if the culture in our group hadn't changed.

The only way we are going to grow, the only way we can push past our comfort zone, is to have people around us who are willing to let us know when our decisions have gone off the rails. However, the only way to ensure we surround ourselves with those people is to embrace the negative criticism and reward them when they are authentic enough to tell us the truth, even if we don't want to hear what they have to say.

I feel fortunate that I could change a negative culture into a positive by merely setting the expectations of what I required and being honest enough to act on those beliefs.

PRINCIPLE #5 – YOU ARE THE PERSON YOU ARE LOOKING TO BECOME

Let your life be shaped by the decisions you made, not by the ones you didn't or that others made for you.

I HAVE ALWAYS BEEN A FAN OF WESTERN MOVIES AND TELEVISION shows. When I was a young boy, my parents would let me stay up and watch *Gunsmoke*, or *Maverick*, or my favorite, *Wild Wild West*.

In 1993, the movie *Tombstone* was released. The principal characters in the movie are Wyatt Earp and John "Doc" Holliday. Wyatt was a lawman most of his life, and Doc, who was a dentist by trade and suffered from tuberculosis, was more or less a gambler and gunfighter.

Toward the end of the movie, there is a scene where Doc is dying in a sanitarium in Glenwood Springs, Colorado. At this point in his life, Wyatt is destitute; he has no money, job, or prospects for a job. But he comes every day to visit Doc, and the two men play cards to pass the time. (In real life, Wyatt didn't learn of Holliday's death until two months after he was buried.)

In this rather poignant exchange, the two men are discussing what they want out of life. Doc explains that he was in love with his cousin when he was young, but she joined a convent over the affair. She was all he ever wanted.

Doc then turns to Wyatt and asks, "What do you want, Wyatt?" Wyatt's response is, "I just want to lead a normal life." To which Doc replies, "There's no normal, there's just life. And get on with living yours."

We should all be looking for the life that we were born to live. Some of us find that life right away, while others search for a lifetime only to seize their purpose at a later age. Still, many others either give up or never bother to look for that reason.

Regardless of which category you fall under, many of us spend a lot of time searching for the person we are supposed to become. The critical thing to remember is that you **are** the person you are looking to become. Even if you haven't found that person yet, you **are** still that person.

Many people spend a good portion of their lives refusing to make decisions that directly impact them, or living with the consequences of the decisions that others have made for them. Why would anyone abdicate the responsibility of leading their uncommon and extraordinary life to someone else?

I want my life to be shaped by the decisions I made, not by the ones others made for me.

As I mentioned previously, basketball was an essential part of my life growing up, and I accepted a scholarship to play college basketball at The Citadel. However, The Citadel was not my initial choice for college.

My first choice was to attend the University of Toledo in the MidAmerican Conference. I had been on a visit to the Toledo campus and was impressed with the new arena that was recently built for the team, and with the players and the coaches. Toledo was a little over two hundred miles from Chicago. That was close enough for my family and friends to travel on weekends to watch me play.

During my visit to the campus, I had the opportunity to meet the president of the university and some business school faculty members, since my father had convinced me I should major in business. As a seventeen-year-old, somewhat sheltered kid, I was impressed with everyone I met and could visualize myself playing at the school. But in all honesty, I had no idea what I wanted to study in college or even where I wanted to continue playing basketball. With three knee surgeries under my belt, I was happy with anyone who would offer me a scholarship.

After the visit, I met with the head and the assistant coach who had coordinated my visit, and was offered a full scholarship to become a member of the Toledo Rockets' basketball program the following season. I thanked the coaches for the offer and expressed my interest in playing at Toledo, but I told them I wanted to talk this opportunity over with my parents, and I would let them know my decision in a few days.

I was extremely excited to have my first college scholarship offer and never realized that more would follow, including an opportunity to play at West Point, Kent State, and The Citadel.

After returning from the visit and talking with my parents, I decided to attend the University of Toledo. I let the coaches know my choice. While I was excited about my first college scholarship offer, I wasn't as happy as I thought I should be. The payoff for all the time spent practicing, strength training, and working in the classroom—not to mention the rehab after those knee surgeries—should have caused absolute euphoria. This was what I had been dreaming of and working for my entire life, the opportunity to play NCAA Division I college basketball, and have my college education paid. But my decision to attend the University of Toledo didn't bring me the unbridled happiness I expected.

Shortly after I verbally accepted the scholarship at Toledo, I received a phone call from the assistant coach. He explained that they weren't sure they had a scholarship for me (even though they had made the offer, and I had accepted). He told me he would let me know in a week or so if the scholarship was still available.

Approximately two weeks later, the assistant coach called and advised that the University did have the scholarship to offer me. I was a little taken aback by the conversation. The coach acted like it was business as usual, to be offering me the scholarship again. I thanked him for the tender but never said I accepted it.

When the phone call concluded, my father asked what transpired. I told him that Toledo offered the scholarship again, so I guess that is where I was going to college.

My dad was much more worldly than I was and asked how I felt about being offered a scholarship, having it put on hold, and then having it offered again? I told him I hadn't given it much thought. I would have been disappointed if they had come back to me and said they were no longer offering to pay for my education, but since that didn't happen, I was good with it.

He then asked me why I thought they had called after they initially offered the scholarship to tell me they weren't sure they had a scholarship for me. When I told him I didn't know, he intimated that more than likely, they had found another player they wanted more than me. During the two weeks I hadn't heard from Toledo, the coaches were likely attempting to recruit this other player. When he turned them down, they came back to me with the scholarship. Dad then asked the central question, did I want to play for someone who offered me a scholarship, took it away, and then offered it again, especially in light of my knee problems?

Still being rather immature, I hadn't considered Dad's question, so I told him I wanted to think about it. I remember not sleeping much that night as I contemplated all the ramifications of what had just occurred

on ESPN in 1982, but other than that, none of my family or friends ever saw me play in college.

I've often wondered how much divine providence had in my decision to attend The Citadel. In hindsight, I learned so much more and matured much faster at The Citadel than I would have at any of the MidAmerica Conference schools.

I saw myself as a Division I basketball player, even after three knee surgeries. And by searching for the person I was looking to become; I realized my dream of playing college basketball.

I could have rolled the dice and seen what would have happened if I attended the University of Toledo. But by deciding to play for someone with character and integrity, like Coach Les, I was able to have a positive college experience, receive a business administration degree, but most importantly, learn about myself. I just wished I had been a better player for Coach Les. He was someone who deserved the best, and I'm not sure he got it from me. I spent too much time in my head instead of enjoying playing a game I loved.

Becoming the person you are supposed to be isn't necessarily a comfortable journey. Many complicated decisions need to be made to discover yourself. If I just look at the choices I had to make to transition from a high school student to a college basketball playing adult, many things were changing in my life, and those changes frightened me a great deal of the time.

While most of my friends were filling out college applications, I focused on taking trips and deciding where I found the best fit for my basketball abilities. Like it or not, basketball was my priority. Only after finding the right "athletic fit," did I look at the college's academic reputation.

Because my college process was so different than my peers, I spent a significant amount of time on my own. I couldn't talk about my experiences with my friends because they didn't understand where I was coming from. As I felt isolated from my buddies, I was becoming more and more comfortable being alone with these heady decisions.

As I mentioned previously, when I was coaching high school basketball, I used to tell my players that they needed to become comfortable with being uncomfortable. I realize they thought that meant just on the basketball court, but it was far more reaching than just sports.

When Toledo took away the scholarship they had offered, I was very uncomfortable, mostly because I didn't have a backup school. But once I decided to move on from Toledo and had methodically worked with my Dad to identify a new (and ultimately better) college, I learned how to live with being uncomfortable. That lesson has helped me throughout my life and had such an impact that it was one of the lessons I wanted to teach my players as a coach.

As I've said, I wasn't a very worldly seventeen-year-old. But the far-reaching impact of where I went to college was always nagging at me. I can't say I spent a great deal of time dwelling upon it, but I knew where I went to college would have a significant bearing on everything I did after I graduated. Although I didn't spend much time considering it, I felt the urgency of wanting to make the correct decision.

When our daughter, Mikela, was considering where she wanted to go to college, basketball was also a consideration. However, for years, my wife and I had been preaching to her that basketball was a means to an end, and that end was to get into the best academic institution that was interested in her. As a result of that influence, the basketball schools she was considering were academically superior to anything I was looking at, except for possibly Army.

Her original inclination was to play at Division III University of Rochester in New York. However, when the Air Force Academy allowed her to play Division I basketball, and get an excellent education to boot, she understood the importance of seizing that opportunity for her future.

While finding the person you are meant to be can be a time rich in growth and development, it is also a time where an important and challenging decision must be made. Many people I've observed abdicate the responsibility for their future to others. They refuse to be accountable for choosing their destiny. They don't understand the growth that a person undergoes when they take charge of the choices that will impact the rest of their life.

I've also noticed that these individuals appear to have the victim mentality, where they blame their lot in life on others. I guess you can do that when you haven't taken responsibility for how your life has turned out. Unfortunately, making a decision is a choice, so is letting someone else choose for you.

The responsibility for altering your life is entirely up to **YOU**. Whining, complaining, and blaming others for your circumstance will not enhance your experience.

I can promise three obstacles will most likely occur along the journey of looking for the person you are supposed to become. All three of these obstacles happened to me during my journey through cancer:

1. Unexpected bad things are going to happen. You just need to let them go and focus on your desired outcome. I was ninety days from being considered cancer-free when a routine scraping of the area around the skin graft on my foot showed the cancer had returned in the same place it initially presented. Almost five years of being on Interferon and continually feeling like I had the flu were for nothing. I had no choice but to ignore the previous five years and re-engage in fighting the disease.

2. Setbacks will occur along your journey. You need to ignore them and continue to push forward. When I learned the cancer had returned, it was suggested I try a biologic therapy of a two-drug cocktail that would do nothing to the cancer but would hopefully rev-up my immune system to fight the melanoma. I had four infusions of this medication, which left me exhausted after each infusion, before realizing it had no impact on the disease. That left my only treatment option being the amputation of most of my left foot.

3. Life will not be fair to you. You need to focus on your goal and forget about how unfair things appear. I had done everything "right" in my life. I never smoked, abused drugs, and rarely drank alcohol. I exercised at least five days a week. I ate nutrient-rich foods with plenty of fruits and vegetables, and I saw my doctor every year for a physical exam and did what he or she recommended in terms of follow-up testing. And yet, I was still afflicted with this rare form of cancer. It simply wasn't fair. But nobody ever promised that life would be fair. I'm reminded of the quote I heard some time ago, "The only thing that makes life unfair is the delusion that it should be fair."

Motivation alone will not cause you to progress. **YOU** have to want to make the decisions and commit to searching for who you are looking for every minute of every day. There are no days off when attempting to make significant and lasting progress in your life.

PRINCIPLE #6 – PUT YOUR GOD AND YOUR FAMILY BEFORE EVERYTHING ELSE

Because, in the end, they will always be there for you.

As part of separate rulings in 1962 and 1963, the United States Supreme Court effectively removed Bible readings and prayer from public schools because of the prohibition of the First Amendment against the enactment of any law "respecting an establishment of religion." In 2005, a federal judge in California ruled that reciting the Pledge of Allegiance in public schools was unconstitutional. The judge claimed the reference to "under God" violated school children's right to be free from coercive requirements to affirm God. In 2017, the United States Supreme Court sided with a lower court ruling ordering a New Mexico city to remove a Ten Commandments monument from outside City Hall.

I understand that the United States was founded on the concept of religious freedom; that no person shall be forced to subscribe to a particular religion or belief; that we are all free to worship the god of our choosing or no god at all. But when did God become a four-letter word? Why are we so afraid to acknowledge or even mention the possible existence of a supreme being?

When was the last time you took a good look at our planet? To see the miracles that present every day. To view the beauty of the sun rising over the mountainous cliffs of the Santa Barbara shoreline. To watch a herd of elk plow their way through waist-deep snow on the Colorado foothills. To view the Spanish moss hanging from the oak trees on a South Carolina plantation. To observe the miracle of birth as a new life, with endless possibilities, struggles from the womb yearning to breathe free. Each one of these precious miracles leaves me in awe. As potent and powerful as we like to believe the human race to be, there is no way our destructive forces would have gotten us this far without the guiding hand of a divine being.

My faith has always been important to me. When I attended Catholic grade school, I was an altar server at Mass. During high school, I was part of the senior service program at Marist that helped those less fortunate in the community. When I was in college, I tried to attend daily Mass. During my senior year, I was elected to the position of president of The Citadel Religious Council.

The Religious Council was an inter-denominational group made up of all the organized religions on campus. Its purpose was to promote the services and activities of every religious organization. It was a council of inclusion, not one of exclusion.

The regimental chaplain was a Catholic priest we all referred to as Father Sam because his Italian last name was hard to pronounce and even more challenging to spell. Father Sam made it a point to make a personal connection with everyone he came in contact with, and I learned a great deal working with him.

One of Fr. Sam's tenets was the importance of ensuring all the denominations on campus felt included on the council. With The Citadel being located in the middle of the Bible Belt, that primarily included the non-Christian faiths such as the Muslims and Jews.

I was elected to my position on The Religious Council at the end of my Junior year, but my tenure didn't begin until senior year. A few weeks after I was elected, I was eating a quick dinner in the Coward Mess Hall on a steamy Friday evening. I had a date in about an hour, and I still needed to shower and get dressed. Just as I was finishing my meal, Tim, who had been elected first vice president on the Religious Council, came over looking very harried. He said he needed to talk to me right away. I explained that I had a date that evening and still needed to get ready. Unfortunately, he persisted in the need to speak to me immediately. Although I was slightly annoyed, I told him to meet me in my room in twenty minutes, and we could talk while I was getting dressed. He readily agreed.

I quickly hurried back to Padgett Thomas Barracks, got undressed, headed down the gallery to the communal showers, and took one of our famous Citadel thirty-second showers, as I was running very late.

When I arrived back at my room, Tim sat at my desk, leafing through one of my business textbooks. I again informed him that I was in a hurry and asked if this discussion could be put off until tomorrow. He assured me it could not.

I told him he had as much time as it would take me to get dressed, which wasn't very long. One thing you learn attending a military college is how to change quickly. As I was toweling off and getting dressed in my blazer uniform, Tim, who was Southern Baptist, proceeded to light into a litany of reasons why he believed that his religion was the faith that every Christian denomination should follow. He then requested that any time a non-Christian sect wanted to promote an event or service on campus, I should send them to see him, and he could explain why they were wrong, per the Bible.

I was furious that he had made me even tardier for my date because he was attempting to propagate his beliefs on others. While I wanted to have a few choice words for him, I managed to curb my tongue and explain the purpose of the Religious Council was to promote all denominations, not just the ones with which we agreed. I further advised that while the Bible certainly was the Word of God, it was written by men, and not everything in it was to be interpreted literally.

As a result of this conversation, I canceled all Religious Council meetings when I was out of town for basketball games. Tim would have filled in for me during those times, and I didn't want to give him the slightest opportunity to offend any of the other religious representatives on the Council.

Religious tolerance has always been important to me. I was raised that discrimination, in any form, is wrong. Being tolerant of another's faith was the underlying purpose of the Religious Council. By promoting each denomination, the council provided every religion the opportunity to learn and understand what and why others believed the way they did. It brought a belief in God down to a human level so that even if we didn't share the faith of another, we could appreciate the importance and the significance of every faith journey.

However, I hoped that we could be more than just tolerant by learning about the different faiths. Tolerance is passive and requires little effort on our part. Even if we disagreed with their faith, loving and accepting each other demanded an active involvement and willingness to open our hearts and minds to include others.

My Catholic faith has always provided me with the stability I needed during difficult times. While I can't scientifically prove that God exists, there have been so many events where His imprint was stamped all over my life. His love and guidance have always been there for me when I was able to still my mind and heart long enough to hear His quiet voice. I'm sure I've missed many of His messages because I was too "me" focused.

In January 2018, I had most of my left foot amputated. My melanoma had returned, and the biologic medication I was given before the amputation did nothing to stunt the disease. While I still had my ankle and my heel, everything in front of my ankle was gone.

It took a few months for the incision to heal. Once that happened, I was sent to physical therapy to learn how to walk again. In the meantime, I felt I was at a crossroads in my life. I wasn't sure where to go next. For the first time I could remember I had no plans, no goals, and no objectives.

I would lie in bed at night, looking up at the ceiling and asking God what He wanted me to do next. I don't know what I was expecting to happen, but God never came right out and told me what to do. There is an old joke that goes; when we talk to God, it's called prayer; when God speaks to us, it's called schizophrenia. But that was what I was hoping would happen. I wanted God to *tell* me what to do directly. That never happened.

What did happen was more of an indirect approach to my next task. Several people close to me suggested I write a book about my cancer journey. Each time the book was recommended, I would dismiss it because I wasn't a writer.

After numerous people made the same book suggestion, I assumed this wasn't just a proposition, but more encouragement from God to write about everything I had been through during the previous six years of cancer treatment.

Believing this was the direction God wanted me to take with my life, I sat down in front of my desktop computer and thought about how I should go about writing my cancer memoir. I decided I would begin writing with just two rules. Rule #1 was that I would write a minimum of one page every day. Rule #2 was that I wouldn't edit any of my work until the first draft of the manuscript had been completed. And that is what I did. I was able to access all my medical records from MD Anderson Cancer Center in Houston and at the University of Colorado Hospital in Denver.

After investing almost a year of my life, I finished the manuscript with 414 pages and over 118,000 words. Even though I had put the facts down on paper, I knew it still needed to be professionally edited.

Thinking that if I could get a publishing company to take an interest in my book, I was sure it would get the tender loving editing care it needed, I attempted the traditional route of querying agents to see if they would pitch my book to a publisher. After contacting over 300 agents who specialized in the memoir genre, I was turned down by all 150 agents that took the time to respond. All of them gave me the same reason: publishers aren't interested in a manuscript about cancer unless you are famous or have a large platform.

After the fiftieth rejection, I had a long talk with God. I couldn't understand why He had me spend a year writing a book nobody seemed to want to publish, let alone read. It wasn't just a book; it was a volume. The average word count of a nonfiction book is between 50,000 and 75,000 words. My memoir was almost double that.

Unfortunately, I never received a direct or indirect response to my heavenly query. Was all that effort a waste of time? I don't think so. I believe I was supposed to write the book. I expected to get it published, but I guess God had other thoughts. God never recommended I *publish* a book; all He suggested was that I *write* the book.

However, I don't feel that year was a waste of time. Putting my experience down on paper was cathartic. It allowed me to recreate my journey over again but from a safe distance that was less frightening and intimidating. It allowed me to examine my emotions and how I physically reacted to all the setbacks that occurred during my journey. It allowed me the opportunity to remember how I treated people who were trying to help me.

As I think back on all those nights staring at the ceiling and contemplating what God wanted, I realized that what I was doing was praying. But being Catholic, I had been instructed how to pray formally. I was taught the Our Father, the Hail Mary, the Glory Be, and the prayer to my guardian angel. Eventually, I was taught how to pray the rosary. However, all these prayers were formal ways of talking to God.

I remembered the scripture verse from Matthew 6:7 that states: *"And when you pray, don't be like those who don't know God. They continue saying things that mean nothing, thinking that God hears them because of their many words."*

I still pray for about an hour every morning. Most, if not all, of that prayer, is formal prayers. I was under the impression that the volume of prayer mattered. That God would bless me more because I spent so much time engaged in reciting proper litanies.

However, if you think about it, you don't spend time with an intimate friend or family member, engaged in formal dialogue. It's much less stuffy and more off-the-cuff and from the heart.

During the COVID-19 pandemic and because of my compromised immune system, I wasn't able to attend Mass in a church. As a result, I used to watch the daily Mass broadcast on my iPad. A priest in Pennsylvania offered one of the Masses I enjoyed. During the portion of the Service where the congregation would typically receive Holy Communion, this priest would tell us to picture ourselves sitting in the lap of Jesus and feel the loving arms of Christ surrounding us. He asked us to put our head on the chest of the Lord and listen to His sacred heartbeat, and every time the heart of Jesus would beat, he would tell us to imagine that Jesus would say, "I love you."

That image, of resting in the loving arms of our Lord and Savior, was amazingly comforting and peaceful. This intimate relationship started me thinking about how I was praying. My prayer was more about how much I was praying, and that would not have been the way I would speak with someone close to me, especially our Creator.

Our prayer with God should be more like how children talk with their parents, no agenda, no scheming, and no pretense. It should come from the heart, and we shouldn't pretend that we are strong and can handle what is going on in our lives, because in many instances, we can't. We should just lay our feelings on the lap of the Lord. Tell Him how we are doing. Tell Him our fears and tribulations. Tell Him our hopes and dreams. But realizing that we may be so overwhelmed with our anxiety, with our guilt, with our stress, that the best we can do is muster his name, God. That simple word, God, coupled with the emotions spilling forth from our heart, has to be one of the most intimate prayers we can ever say.

Drop your issues in His lap and thank Him for the many blessings He has bestowed upon you and the knowledge that He will now be in charge of your problems. That is a much better way to bow yourself before the Lord and commune with His Sacred Heart.

The connection with God provides us the roadmap for our journey. But it is just as important to have others of faith with you as you attempt to navigate your life.

I was so fortunate to have a loving and caring wife and daughter during my cancer journey. They have done so much to help me get through this disease.

When I was a recruit in the Cincinnati Police Academy, our defensive tactics instructor required us to bring a photograph of the people we loved the most to class. We would look at those photos as we learned different techniques to protect ourselves. The reason for the images was that we were taught that we would fight harder for someone we loved than we would fight for ourselves.

Our instructor wanted us to have a visual image imprinted on our minds for the time when we had to use these skills to potentially save our lives on the streets. He needed us to remember who the people were who meant the most to us. Those were the people who loved us and wanted us to come home after our shift.

Having my family top of mind during my cancer experience was something that helped me be more courageous. It helped me knowing that others were looking at how I responded to this experience and might be taking their cues from my actions.

When my father died, his boss, John, attended the wake service. I'll never forget what John told my brother Larry and me. He explained that everyone at the service, and the church and cemetery the following day, would be taking their cues from how we acted. If we were down and depressed, that would be the way the mourners would respond. But if we were positive and upbeat, that was how everyone would feel.

Larry and I put a great deal of stock in what John told us because many years earlier when John and his first wife were raising three young boys, his wife unexpectedly died. He told us how he had to set the tone at the service to comfort his sons and assist all the mourners through this tragic event.

I recall an incident where my wife and daughter rallied around me to get me where I needed to go.

I had just been discharged from the hospital after spending three days recovering from having the lymph nodes in my groin removed and having a skin graft on my left foot. Before I left the hospital, I was offered pain medication, but the ride home was only a few minutes, so I declined the morphine.

Getting my six-foot-eight frame into the car with the forty staples tugging on my groin proved somewhat challenging. After extending my long legs into the front passenger compartment, I achieved a comfortable position in the back seat.

After we arrived home, I managed the three steps into the house from the garage, on my crutches, without much effort. I then needed to traverse seven more steps to a landing, followed by an additional seven steps to make it to the bedroom upstairs. Negotiating the stairs proved to be more of a challenge than I anticipated.

By the time I got to the landing, the staples in my groin were pulling and pinching, making the incision feel like it was on fire. I was in so much pain that I was covered in perspiration and breathing heavily. I implored my family just to let me take a break and sit down on one of the steps. Our daughter, Mikela, would have nothing of it. She knew that if I sat my 240-pound body on the tread, it would be almost impossible to get me moving again, given that the pain was continuing to increase.

Without a second thought, Mikela grabbed my shirt and pulled me from the front as my wife pushed from the back to eventually get me to the top of the stairs, where I collapsed in a wet mess onto the sofa outside the bedroom.

I've often thought about that event and how fortunate I was to have people who cared enough about me to push and pull me to my destination when I wasn't able to make it by myself.

So here is a question for you: Who, in your life, is pushing or pulling you toward your uncommon and extraordinary life? Maybe more importantly, who are you pushing or pulling to help them find and reach their purpose?

We all need positive, encouraging, and caring people to help us in our lives. No matter how determined or resolute we are, from time to time, we need others who aren't afraid to tell us the truth and who guide us along the correct path so we don't diverge down a route that will take us in a direction we don't want to go.

During my cancer journey in Houston, I had a person who would always encourage and help me along this frightening path. His name was Bud. Bud had been an air defense artillery officer in North Africa during World War II. After the war, he returned home and made and sold children's furniture at his factory in New York. After his wife died, his daughter, Jade, brought him to Houston to live with her.

When I met Bud, he was in his nineties but was still very sharp mentally and got around without assistance. Our friendship quickly grew as Bud regaled me with stories from his time as a lieutenant in the army and his business in New York. Both his children were expert tennis players who played on the junior circuit growing up. As adults, they are accomplished physicians.

After my wife, Bud was the first person I called when I learned I had cancer. I wanted to talk to Bud for two reasons. First, he was a good friend and a great listener, and, second, his daughter, Jade, was a neuro-ophthalmologist practicing at MD Anderson Cancer Center.

One thing that perturbed me most about people when they found out I had cancer, or had just had surgery, or was going in for some tests, was a widespread reaction that we have all given at one time or another. The response was, "If you need anything or if there is anything I can do, just let me know."

In my opinion, that response is a dodge! It says you understand my family and I are going through a difficult time, but you aren't getting involved unless I *ask* you for something specific. Never mind that I have numerous things on my plate that I am trying to deal with, on top of being afraid and worried. Sorry, but I just don't have the time to think of ways you can help us, which is precisely what the response is designed to do. Hey, I will offer my assistance and act as a team player, but I know you're too occupied with the here and now to consider anything for me to do to assist you. I offered. You didn't make a suggestion. I am off the hook!

After my first surgery at MD Anderson Cancer Center, I'd just gotten home from the hospital when my cell phone rang. It was a call from Bud. He wanted to know if he could drop by for a few minutes and give us some items he picked up at Costco.

Since I had pretty much settled in, we invited Bud over. Within thirty minutes, my almost hundred-year-old buddy was standing in our house with a pan of cream cheese Danish and a freshly cooked chicken he'd just purchased for us at Costco. Bud loved going to Costco. I think he enjoyed the interaction with all the customers more than the discount shopping. Bud never met a stranger!

Bud didn't ask if we needed anything. Bud didn't take himself off the hook by telling us to call him if he could help. Bud "caused something to happen." We were extremely grateful to have food for breakfast and dinner.

If you are sincerely committed to assisting someone, actually cause something positive to happen in their lives. Don't *ask* others what they need, *tell* them what you're going to do, and then do it. Take some of the burdens off those you care about who desperately need your assistance. People always need food, or to have someone watch the kids, or take the dog for a walk, or cut the grass, or take out the trash. The same day-to-day chores you perform at your house, your family and friends, who are going through a tumultuous time, have to accomplish at their home.

Unfortunately, people don't have time to figure out how you can help them. So, you determine what you are going to do and get involved and get it done. Don't watch from the sidelines and try to convince yourself you are participating in the game.

Relying on the three *F*s, faith, family, and friends, has been indispensable in getting me through the most challenging and difficult portion of my life. Without a doubt, sometime in the future, you will find yourself in my position. You will need the help of others to usher you from this life. Don't be afraid to get involved in the ugly, nasty, and debilitating part of someone's tragedy. You could be the one person that calms their fears and puts their mind at ease. Be that person.

PRINCIPLE #7 – BE PART OF SOMETHING BIGGER THAN YOURSELF

Learn to be a good teammate and realize rock bottom is a good place to start to build the foundation of your life.

LIFE IS MOST LIKELY THE MOST PROMINENT TEAM GAME IN WHICH WE participate. But how do we know what it takes to be a good teammate? How do we learn to sacrifice what is beneficial for ourselves for the betterment of others? How do we discover how to put our egos aside and do what is in the group's best interest?

In my life, I learned many of these lessons by being part of a sports team. Having played organized athletics of one kind or another from the time I was nine years old until I was twenty-one, helped me understand what it meant to be part of something bigger than myself.

It's hard for me to choose my favorite or the most influential teams I've played on, but in looking back on my basketball career, I would have to say my preferred teams were my 1971-72 Kar-Mel Recreation League team and my 1973-74 St. Anthony Parish middle school team.

When I look back at the start of my basketball career, I realize how fortunate I was. I was lucky enough to have played on the same team with my friend Scott. Scott was the point guard on our Kar-Mel Recreation League team, the Royals, in Columbus, Ohio, from 1970 through 1972.

It wasn't that Scott was an outstanding point guard (which he was) that made the team experience so rewarding for me. It was the fact that Scott's dad was the assistant coach for The Ohio State University men's basketball team from 1965 until 1976, during which the Buckeyes won or shared two Big Ten championships.

I vividly remember walking into the small gymnasium at Valley Forge school, which doubled as a lunchroom and an auditorium, behind Scott's dad and the tallest man I had ever seen. That man turned out to be a seven-foot-tall recruit who had to duck to get through the gymnasium doors. This young man would go on to have a successful career at Ohio State and eventually played three years in the National Basketball Association with the Cleveland Cavaliers.

Our 1971–72 team was special to me for several reasons. First off, my dad was our coach. Having your father as your coach can be a double-edged sword as you get to spend time with your father doing something you love, but you can also bear the wrath of your dad when things don't go the team's way. Second, our team, the Royals, was undefeated that season, going a perfect 11-0 and winning the Kar-Mel Championship. Scott and I led the team in scoring averaging 14.5 and 14.0 points per game, respectively. Third, I was able to play on the team with my brother, Larry, for the second year. But the most crucial reason that team was so special was because of what I had learned the season prior and was able to apply this season.

In the previous season, our team had a record of 15-1. We lost a regular-season game to our rivals, the Mustangs, by one point. That was the first loss I had ever suffered on the basketball court, and I took it very hard. So hard, that I was down the hall sobbing when my dad came out of the gym looking for me to go home. I remember him coming up to me and saying, "What are you crying for?"

I guess I was expecting him to put his arm around me and tell me everything was going to be okay. But instead, he showed some tough love. Through my sobs, all I could say to him was I was upset that we had lost. At that point in my life, I didn't know how to lose. Dad matter-of-factly told me I had better get used to defeat because no matter how good you are at your craft, you will fail from time to time. Other teams would have a great night shooting, and you would lose. Your team would experience an injury and not be at 100% strength, and you would lose, or you would just have an off night and lose to an inferior team. Regardless of the reason, life is filled with all kinds of loss and disappointment.

But just because you lose on the scoreboard, doesn't mean you are a loser. You only become a loser when your values aren't aligned with your actions, such as when you refuse to show good sportsmanship after a game. You only become a loser when you continuously focus on the negative aspect of competition and can't see the value of pursuing a goal with your teammates. You only become a loser when you think the team revolves around you, and you refuse to sacrifice yourself for the betterment of the group. You only become a loser when you decline to respect yourself or others by refusing to support your teammates who are doing their best. You only become a loser when you give up on yourself or the team because things aren't going your way. You only become a loser when you refuse to take responsibility for your actions or your teammates' actions, such as when you look to blame others or pass the buck for the mistakes you have committed. You only become a loser when you think you are more significant than the team. And being a loser will prevent any amount of success from coming your way and from having others wanting you to be part of their journey.

A person isn't born a loser. People become losers because they experience significant failure in their lives, aren't mature enough to learn the lessons a defeat can teach, or circumstances pile up against them, and they hit rock bottom.

But rock bottom can be a great place to start laying the foundation for a better life. Unfortunately, many people can't get off the bottom once they're there and let their bad luck or misfortune define who they are. Everyone makes mistakes; that's how we learn and grow. But you aren't a loser until you start blaming others for those mistakes.

That is the great thing about team sports, no matter how bad things get or how awful you are playing, you have others around to support you.

Dad didn't impart all that wisdom to my little brain. But he did help me to understand that the world didn't revolve around me, especially when I was part of a team.

Our team, the Royals, had been the premier team in the Valley Forge Recreation League. We had won the league championship for the previous two seasons, and everyone wanted to beat us when we played —every opponent brought their best effort when competing against us. We had to be ready every night. There were no easy games for us.

But winning breeds winning, just as losing breeds losing. If your team can find a way to win, that sets a standard and, I believe, gives you an advantage when you are in a tight game, whether that game is on the basketball court or in your life. When it comes down to it, teams (or people) that know how to win have a decided advantage over organizations that don't understand what it takes to be winners.

My second favorite team was my 1973-74 St. Anthony School Parish, eighth-grade team. Our "Mustang" team went 30-3 and won the Boys Basketball of America Ohio and National titles.

I chose this team as one of my favorites because we were a ragtag group of guys who came together to do our best at a sport we enjoyed. Everyone checked their egos at the door. It didn't matter how many points you scored or how many rebounds you got. What mattered was doing your best and having fun.

When I say we were a ragtag group, I emphasize that by looking at our uniforms. Our school colors were gold and black. We didn't have home or away uniforms. We had simple gold jerseys and shorts with black numbers on them. By looking at us, you would have no idea what team we were because there was no school name anywhere on our uniforms. There wasn't even a team logo on the uniforms.

Also, our school didn't have a gymnasium. We had to practice wherever our coach found us a gym. That was usually at the local Catholic high school, St. Francis De Sales. The only problem with practicing at De Sales was we had to wait until all the high school teams had finished their workouts before we could use the gym. That meant practice was usually scheduled for 7:00 p.m.

Along with being our head coach, Mr. Mackessy was the designated carpool driver. I remember my mom dropping us off at the Mackessy house, which was right next to Northland High School, and being chauffeured to De Sales in their white station wagon. When we arrived at the high school, we were the only car in the parking lot, and the school was dark inside. Even the janitor had gone home by the time we were practicing.

I still recall the gymnasium's earthy smell, a mix of a topical analgesic and sweat. We had no access to the locker room, so we unpacked our gym bags against the wall and quickly changed into our practice uniforms. Given that we were a Catholic school, our practice uniforms were more angelic than anything else. Mr. Mackessy required a plain white T-shirt, white gym shorts, white socks, and gym shoes. Our footwear predated shoes specifically designed for basketball.

I loved going to practice and learning about the game and how my role influenced the team. Although I was the tallest player on the team at six foot four, and averaged the most points, I was very unsure of myself. I was tall but extremely skinny; some might even describe me as wiry. I wore a size thirteen shoe, and my coordination hadn't caught up with my body yet.

Fortunately, I was accepted by my teammates for who I was, not for who they wanted me to be.

Our team won the Catholic Diocese of Columbus De Sales League with a perfect record of 9-0. In the Catholic City Playoffs, we dominated Corpus Christi, Immaculate Conception, and Pope John XXIII to cap an undefeated season in the Columbus Catholic League at 12-0.

In the Boys Basketball of America Regional Playoffs, we finished with a record of 6-1 and advanced to the state championship round. We beat a team from Grove City who had beaten us twice during the regular season, once by thirty-four points. Winning the Ohio Championship was fantastic. The team trophy we received was taller than some of the players we had on our team!

Winning the Ohio tournament qualified our team for the National Tournament in Cincinnati, Ohio, on March 30 and 31, 1974. In 1974, traveling out of your area to play a middle school basketball game wasn't done. There were no traveling or AAU teams back then.

But the excitement of having all my teammates and their families at a local Holiday Inn in Cincinnati was exhilarating. I believe I was more interested in hanging out with my teammates than I was in playing basketball.

We advanced to the National Championship game by beating another team from Kentucky on a Saturday afternoon. Our excitement of making it to the championship game the next afternoon was bittersweet. We felt fortunate to be playing for this prestigious honor but also knew it would be the last game we were all together. For the first time all season, I didn't sleep well the night before this big game. I wasn't anxious, but I found myself reliving the exhilaration of the season. No one had ever expected the "Thundering Herd" from a little parish in Columbus to have the success we had on the court that season. It was like living in a dream, but I got to do it with a group of guys that I loved.

The following afternoon, in an obscure Reading High School gymnasium in Cincinnati with only our families in attendance, I hit a turnaround baseline jump shot with twenty-seven seconds left to secure the win over a team from Maysville, Kentucky, to give St Anthony the Boys Basketball of America National Championship. The final score was 33-32.

The exhilaration I felt after the victory was unbelievable. Our enthusiasm ran rampant. After the win, we were hugging everyone we came in contact with; parents, teammates, cheerleaders all experienced the sweaty hugs from a true champion.

I was named to the all-tournament team along with my teammates John Solinger and Steve Rowe. I was further honored by being selected to the All-American squad. The individual accolades were nice, but nothing compared to closing out our season on such a high note with a great group of players, coaches, family, and fans.

Our success on the court was written about in the *Columbus Dispatch, The Catholic Times, The Neighborhood News*, and our *St Anthony Parish Bulletin*. The team was further honored with an achievement award from the Columbus Agonis Club. We were also acknowledged with Columbus City Council Resolution 89X-74 and attended the City Council meeting to receive the proclamation. I also received a proclamation from the Ohio State Senate congratulating me on my selection to the Boys Basketball of America All-American team.

Our season came to an official close on Sunday, April 28, 1974, with our Basketball Banquet, held at the historic Worthington Inn.

The team members I had such a pleasure playing with were: John Solinger, John Meister, Scott Funk, John Mackessy, Jim Dickhause, Lou Tiberi, Steve Rowe, Greg Diehl, John Prince, Nick Capparuccini, and Jerry Savage. Dick Mackessy was our head coach, and my dad, Jack Tucker, was our assistant coach. I have an eight-by-ten black-and-white team photo taken outside the Worthington Inn with the National Championship trophy. It is a photo I cherish deeply.

Sometimes being part of something bigger than yourself has nothing to do with sports or a team. Occasionally it means sacrificing your life for the betterment of another. One season when I played on the Royals in the Kar-Mel league, I had a teammate named David.

David wasn't a good player. Basketball wasn't something he had a passion for, but he always showed up and gave his best in practices and games. I respected him for the effort he put forward.

I wasn't close with David while we were teammates. He went to a different school and lived in Forest Park West, while my family lived in Forest Park East.

Shortly after college, I reconnected with David after relocating to the Columbus, Ohio, area. I found David to be in a declining state of health. His diabetes had robbed him of his eyesight. His mom, Lee, was solely responsible for his medical care and all his basic needs. Lee was widowed, and her other children had their own lives scattered around Columbus but would help with David's care when they were able.

I would occasionally visit with David to free his mom up to run errands and take some time for herself. David's life was relatively simple. His hobby was acquiring miniature soldiers from all different wars throughout history. He used some of his monthly disability check to pay someone to paint the metal figures with the appropriate uniform colors and insignia. He had shelves filled with these action figures representing warriors from as far back as the French *Grande Armée* commanded by Napoleon to the Vietnam Era U.S. Army Forces led by General William Westmoreland.

David spent a great deal of time on his hobby and had various sight-impaired devices that made life a little better for a young man who was mostly confined to his room in the basement of the split-level home he shared with his mom on Thurell Road in Columbus.

When I say David's mom was his sole caregiver, she alone was responsible for all of David's medical needs. She was the only person

David trusted to continually monitor his blood sugar levels. She drove him to every doctor's appointment and was an encyclopedia of information on all his medical issues. She knew what worked and what didn't and wouldn't let a new doctor come anywhere near her son until he or she was fully briefed on David's medical conditions. Her awareness and knowledge of David's health issues and the treatments that worked best for him were on par with many of the physicians who treated him.

This constant vigilance to her son's care came at a price. She rarely got a day off. She never took a vacation or was able to go out with friends. The family would come over if there were a holiday or special occasion, but David seldom traveled outside the house for anything other than a medical appointment.

Over the years, Lee began looking haggard and worn down as she sat in her tiny kitchen, smoking unfiltered cigarette after cigarette. But she had a dogged dedication to her son that I admired. David appeared to be her sole purpose for living.

When my wife and I got married and moved to California, I lost touch with David. I would call him a few times a year to check up on him, but I would never see my friend again. For some time in late 2004, I made several attempts to call David on the phone. After being unable to get in touch with him, in the spring of 2005, I sent him a letter. Several weeks later, I received a response from his mom. She explained that David had developed an infection in his legs as a result of his diabetes. The standard oral antibiotic treatments were started, but they didn't affect the infection. Eventually, David was hospitalized to stem the toxicity with stronger intravenous medication. When that failed to improve his health, his legs were amputated. The contagion weakened him to the point that the infection spread in his body and took his life. His mom wrote that she attempted to contact me but didn't have my address or phone number. She enclosed David's obituary that was printed in the *Columbus Dispatch*.

While I was saddened that David's life had ended and I wasn't able to say goodbye to my friend, I was more concerned with how his mother, who had committed her entire existence to her son's care, would handle this massive void in her life. I stayed in contact with Lee for almost a year, until I called and the phone was disconnected. Several months later, I learned she had sold the house, but I would never talk with her again.

I don't know the criteria for sainthood, but I think Lee would qualify. Here was a woman with her own significant financial and health challenges, who spent all her time and attention on her son's persistent and single-minded care. I never heard her complain or say anything disparaging about David or his medical conditions. She never pitied her circumstance or whined about the road she was traveling. I admired her devotion to something bigger than herself: her tenacious commitment and unconditional love toward her son.

I don't doubt that Lee has been called to her eternal rest. I'm sure God will make sure her heavenly existence is much more pleasurable than her one on earth.

Does being part of something bigger than yourself preclude that self from being you?

I recall the story of a young woman diagnosed with dyslexia, an attention disorder, and an anxiety disorder between seventh and eighth grades. Her teachers were alerted to a potential problem when they saw that she understood the material in class but couldn't effectively transfer that knowledge during exams.

Eventually, it was recommended her parents have her tested for any potential learning issues. This testing involved many days of performing various exercises and exams and included in-depth interviews with her parents.

When her learning challenges were diagnosed, she was entitled to extra time on her exams, and took those tests in a separate room to avoid distractions.

It was further recommended that her parents sign her up with a learning specialist to determine the best methods that she could use to improve her studying. The learning specialist helped this young girl to use colors and music when studying. She also suggested she use lined graph paper to assist with keeping her numbers in the proper columns when learning math and science.

Throughout middle and high school, this student refined her learning strategies and became a member of the National Honor Society during her senior year in high school.

Because of her ability to play basketball, she was offered an opportunity to go to college and play basketball at the United States Air Force Academy. Because of the Academy's emphasis on math and science courses, coupled with this student's learning issues, she was sent the Academy's prep school to see if she could handle the rigors of an Academy education. Despite her learning diagnosis, the Air Force Academy didn't provide the accommodations the law required she be given in high school. The prep school was an opportunity to determine if she could handle the rigorous academic workload at the Academy.

After excelling at the prep school, she was admitted to the Air Force Academy the following year, as a member of the class of 2019.

Despite a knee operation that forced her to give up her basketball career after her freshman season, she went on to excel academically and militarily at the Academy. She made Dean's List several semesters, despite taking courses that focused on aeronautical engineering, astro-engineering, chemical, electrical engineering, and chemistry and physics.

She also held several leadership positions within her squad and volunteered her expertise as a basketball coach at the local YMCA.

On a sunny May 30, 2019 morning, she walked across the stage at Falcon Stadium, received her diploma, and shook hands with the President of the United States.

Obtaining her Bachelor of Science degree in behavioral science, along with a religious studies minor, was the culmination of an academic career filled with challenges and pitfalls that were overcome to make this young lady a person who became bigger than anyone ever imagined she could be.

I am filled with pride when I recall this story because the young lady in question is our daughter, Mikela. As her parents, my wife and I are congratulated continuously for Mikela's graduation from one of the most challenging colleges in the country. My reply to these accolades is always, "Don't congratulate us, Mikela did all the heavy lifting."

If there was ever a person who took on the challenge of becoming something bigger than herself, it was Mikela. Regardless of the outcome, no parents could be any prouder than Roberta and I are of our daughter.

Research has shown that being connected to something larger than ourselves makes our lives more prosperous and fulfilled. This association helps us to find and live our uncommon and extraordinary purpose. It guides and shapes our values and priorities and provides us with a touchstone when facing adversity.

Being part of groups with rich traditions, focused on achieving excellence for the overall betterment of the group, was how I learned that the true meaning in life was so much more significant and impactful than just what was happening in my life.

Associating with things greater than ourselves has a positive impact on our lives. It produces the ripple effect of touching the lives of so many people around us, in many instances, people we don't even know.

While some say we are only responsible for ourselves, I believe the impact of our lives has the unforeseen ability to influence all humanity's souls. How we choose to live our lives will be our legacy.

Since, to one degree or another, we are all allowed to participate in the game of life, shouldn't we rise from our common and ordinary lives and grab the glory that will not only lead us to fulfillment, but inspire others to pursue their uncommon and extraordinary lives?

PRINCIPLE #8 – FAIL OFTEN, ESPECIALLY WHEN YOU ARE YOUNG

Take smart, calculated chances, and learn from your mistakes. Take responsibility for your errors, and don't be afraid to apologize.

IT'S EASY TO SAY THAT PEOPLE SHOULD FAIL, BUT NOBODY PURPOSELY sets out to flop. People fail for several reasons. Many people fail because they lack the confidence to succeed, or are frightened of obtaining what they are trying to achieve. Others fail because they don't care enough to put in the effort to be successful, or because they are in the wrong place at the wrong time. But I believe most people fail because they quit or give up. If people can learn from their missteps, they can often turn their failure into success.

There is a marked difference between someone who fails and someone who quits. People fail at things every day. However, if you view failure as the end of your journey, then you are a quitter. People who fail see the misstep as part of the learning process. They learn from their mistakes, and apply that knowledge improving on their idea. As

Thomas Edison once said, "I have not failed. I've just found 10,000 ways that don't work."

I recall a poem I heard long ago about the importance of never giving up. It was written by the American Quaker poet and abolitionist John Greenleaf Whittier, and goes like this:

> When things go wrong as they sometimes will,
> When the road you're trudging seems all uphill,
> When the funds are low, and the debts are high,
> And when you want to smile, but you have to sigh,
> When care is pressing you down a bit –
> Rest if you must, but don't you quit.
>
> Life is queer with its twists and turns,
> As every one of us sometimes learns,
> And many a fellow turns about
> When he might have won had he stuck it out.
> Don't give up though the pace seems slow—
> You may succeed with another blow.
>
> Often the goal is nearer than
> It seems to a faint and faltering man;
> Often the struggler has given up
> When he might have captured the victor's cup;
> And he learned too late when the night came down,
> How close he was to the golden crown.
>
> Success is failure turned inside out—
> The silver tint in the clouds of doubt,
> And you never can tell how close you are,
> It might be near when it seems afar;
> So, stick to the fight when you're hardest hit—
> It's when things seem worst that you must not quit.

One of the most important things a person needs to be successful, as well as to fail, is courage.

Nelson Mandela, the former President of South Africa, is quoted as saying, "Courage is not the absence of fear, but the triumph over it."

Every one of us is afraid of something. We are scared of failing. We are frightened of embarrassing ourselves in front of our boss, or our colleagues, or the man or woman we have a crush on. We are fearful of making a mistake and having others find out we aren't perfect.

By failing to pursue our goals or dreams, fear controls us by saying no. No to chasing that new idea. No to looking for a better job. No to pursuing that potential relationship.

But if we dare to face up to our fears and say yes to our goals and desires, even if they don't pan out, that's how we define courage. And if we stand up to our fears once, we are more likely to do it again and again.

By standing up to our fears and insecurities, we dare to attempt new things and potentially live our uncommon and extraordinary life.

I started my business career in the field marketing department at Wendy's. However, I eventually moved to the new product marketing department. Our focus was to develop the advertising materials for any new product the company expanded, including any point of purchase material for products being tested in specific markets.

One of the products that were being considered for implementation was a beef nugget (similar to a chicken nugget). Before any product is tested in the stores, it goes through a rigorous trial of taste testing and focus groups. The initial findings indicated that the beef nugget's flavor was excellent, but the visual appeal was lacking.

The new product development vice president had determined that the product shouldn't go forward with implementation into test stores.

However, his subordinate, the new product development director, was convinced the product would be a huge success among customers if it were only given a chance.

Implementing any new product, even on a small scale in a few stores, is very expensive. The product suppliers must be identified, and a distribution chain established to get the product to the stores. Equipment to cook the product had to be procured and determined where it would be placed in the store. Marketing material needed to be designed and produced. The name of the product had to be determined, and a place on the menu board identified. The store managers and staff had to be trained. A designated key needed to be programmed on the register so sales could be tracked. All these things needed to be implemented for any potential new product. It could cost hundreds of thousands of dollars to determine the viability of a single new menu item.

After some heated discussion, the vice president relented and told the director he could implement beef nuggets in a handful of company stores in the Columbus, Ohio, market, but, "You better be damn sure this is going to work."

Once everything was in place, beef nuggets went live in several of Wendy's restaurants in Columbus. The product was a total disaster. The customers who purchased the nuggets said the flavor was excellent, but the nuggets resembled breaded excrement, and they couldn't get past the lacking visual appeal of the product.

At the end of the three-month testing period, the director was expecting to get a good tongue lashing from his boss, or at worst, be shown the door for his insistence on the beef nugget test implementation.

When all the department representatives convened for the debrief meeting after the beef nugget test was concluded, everyone was more interested in the expected fireworks the vice president was predicted to release on his director. However, we were pleasantly surprised when the VP complimented his subordinate for his convictions. He went on to say that, based on the market and food testing research, he didn't think the product should have moved to the next stage, but he appreciated how his director had stood up for a product he believed had value. While the ultimate decision for whether a product continues on the process is his, he wanted to make sure that the departments responsible for implementing new menu items weren't abdicating their responsibility in fighting for what they thought was right.

Although the director had failed in his assessment of the beef nuggets' profitability, he rolled the dice on a product his gut told him would be lucrative. That was the first time I had ever seen someone stick their neck out in a corporate environment.

When I was a freshman in high school at St. Charles Preparatory School, I was required to take an art appreciation class. Part of the class requirements were that we had to write a report on a famous artist. I chose to write about Vincent Van Gogh because I thought it was interesting that he had cut off part of his left ear.

By all accounts, Van Gogh was a commercial failure as an artist. In the span of approximately ten years, he painted over 2,100 works of art, most of them in the last two years of his life.

Van Gogh started as an art dealer but later became a missionary to help his depression. When he was twenty-eight years old, he began to paint and had to move in with his family and was financially supported by his brother.

When he was thirty-three years old, he moved to Paris to continue painting. During a heated argument with his friend, Impressionist painter Paul Gauguin, Vincent took a razor and severed his left ear.

He had a severe mental illness, including psychosis and delusions. At thirty-seven, he shot himself in the chest, dying two days later from an infection because the bullet was unable to be removed.

Van Gogh is reported to have sold only one painting during his lifetime but is considered one of the foremost artists in modern history.

Dr. Seuss published *Green Eggs and Ham* less than a month after I was born. I remember my parents reading that book to me as I was growing up. As of 2019, over eight million copies of the title have been sold and Dr. Seuss is one of the most recognizable and well-loved authors of children's literature.

But Dr. Seuss, who was born Theodor Seuss Geisel, was not always a successful author and storyteller.

He initially worked as an illustrator after college and produced animated films for the United States military during World War II. His first book was titled *And to Think That I Saw It on Mulberry Street* and was rejected twenty-seven times before being accepted for publication. But the story of how the book came to be published is quite impressive.

Dr. Seuss was walking home from his twenty-seventh rejection in New York City when he happened to run into a classmate from his days at Dartmouth College, Mike McClintock.

That morning, McClintock had just taken the job as editor of children's books at Vanguard Press. McClintock inquired about what Seuss was carrying when Geisel told him it was a children's book that he was unable to get published. Geisel was invited to Vanguard's offices and sold the book to McClintock that day. Vanguard Press sold six million copies of the book. Years later, Dr. Seuss is reported to have said, "If he had been walking down the other side of Madison Avenue, I'd be in the dry-cleaning business today."

On a more personal note, I had never known anyone who was faced with a life and death situation and was put in a position of making a genuinely courageous decision until I met my friend Kathy.

Kathy was born in Gunnison, Colorado, in December 1958. She was a pathologist in the speech therapy department at Riverside Methodist Hospital in Columbus, Ohio, during the 1980s and early 1990s. We met when I was the manager of new programs for the hospital, and Kathy suggested the implementation of a new therapy program to assist those patients afflicted with a stuttering disorder. I assisted Kathy in taking her idea from a concept to a workable service offered by the speech therapy department at Riverside.

As Kathy and I worked on the development of her idea, we became good friends. We realized she and her fiancé, John, lived just a few blocks from my house. John and I were also enrolled in the law school program at Capital University in Columbus. In addition to implementing this new service for her patients, Kathy was occupied with planning her wedding to John.

After the stuttering program was instituted, I would occasionally stop by the speech therapy department to check the progress of the new treatment. Each time I showed up, Kathy would fill me in on all the developments of planning her wedding, and her new therapy technique.

As her wedding day drew closer, the bubbly, continually smiling woman I had come to know began to look tired and worn-down. Kathy spoke of always being fatigued but attributed her exhaustion to her nonstop schedule of planning a large formal wedding while working a full-time job at the hospital.

After Kathy and John returned from their honeymoon, Kathy continued to wrestle with tremendous fatigue and eventually went to her doctor for a checkup. What we had all written off as tiredness from planning a large wedding turned out to be a deadly cancer called chronic myelogenous leukemia, or CML for short. CML is a rare cancer of the bone marrow that causes an increased number of white blood cells to be produced.

Kathy and John were devastated by the news. Still, Kathy continued her daily routine at Riverside while meeting with specialists from around the country to determine her best course of treatment. Eventually, chemotherapy was prescribed as the greatest hope of containing her disease. However, a relatively new procedure, called a bone marrow transplant, was Kathy's only hope for a cure and full recovery.

As Kathy endured the debilitating side effects of her chemotherapy treatment, her immediate family and relatives were screened as possible bone marrow donors. Unfortunately, none would prove to be a suitable match. Kathy approached Riverside's organ and tissue procurement manager, Mary, and me, about holding a bone marrow donor drive. The drive's goal was to find a suitable donor for Kathy and educate the hospital staff and community about this new life-saving procedure. At the same time, the hope was to add as many additional donors as possible to the National Bone Marrow Donor Registry.

One of the biggest impediments to a successful drive was raising the money to cover the cost of testing each individual who desired to be screened. While Riverside was supportive of the drive and provided us with space and personnel, they weren't in a financial position to fund the drive.

It was suggested that I meet with Kathy's father-in-law, Jack, and see if he would be willing to sponsor the drive. We estimated it would cost approximately $25,000 to cover the fees associated with testing the hundreds of people we expected would turn out for the bone marrow drive.

While I thought asking Jack for the money was an excellent idea, I was somewhat intimidated by requesting another person give such a large sum of money. In addition to being Kathy's father-in-law, Jack was the chairman of the board of directors at Riverside and was one of President Richard Nixon's attorneys during the Watergate scandal in the 1970s. He was also a founding partner of the most prestigious law firm in Columbus.

Fortunately, Jack made it very comfortable when I met with him in his office on State Street in downtown Columbus. He was extremely cordial when he greeted me and put me at ease right away. As I laid out the plans for the bone marrow donor drive, he pledged his full support and any funding necessary to make the drive a success.

As Kathy and John worked with Mary and me to organize and fund the bone marrow drive, her chemotherapy had its desired effect, and Kathy's leukemia went into remission. While everyone was encouraged by the report of the disease being retarded, Kathy and her doctors knew it was only a matter of time before the deadly cancer reemerged.

Kathy's physicians gave her an ultimatum. Since the leukemia was in remission and Kathy had regained much of her strength and vitality, it would be ideal for performing the risky bone marrow transplant. If Kathy waited until the cancer reappeared, she might not be strong enough to survive the procedure.

While Riverside Hospital held the first bone marrow donor drive in Central Ohio, Kathy and her new husband faced a tremendous dilemma. Kathy felt great, the best she had in months. Her doctors had located a suitable bone marrow donor for Kathy and wanted to use her improved health and stamina to perform the delicate procedure. If Kathy refused or postponed the transplant, she might not be strong enough to tolerate it and would most likely live another two to three years.

Her plight was quite simple. Kathy could do nothing and have two to three years of quality life with John and her family. Or, she could take an enormous gamble on a relatively new procedure that, if successful, would cure her leukemia. In making this decision, Kathy and John knew full well she had a fifty/fifty chance of surviving the transplant.

In my mind, Kathy made the most courageous decision of anyone I had ever known. She decided to take a chance to live a long, full, and meaningful life with her husband and chose to move forward with the bone marrow transplant.

After isolating Kathy in a sterile environment at The Ohio State University Hospital, her immune system was wiped out with potent doses of chemotherapy. She was taken right to the edge of death before being administered the life-saving marrow harvested from an anonymous donor. Initially, after receiving the new bone marrow, Kathy's blood counts and energy level began to improve. We were hopeful that Kathy was on the road to a full recovery which included eradicating her leukemia.

As time moved on, Kathy developed severe complications when her body began to turn on itself and reject the donated marrow. The doctors tried everything in their arsenal to reverse the graft versus host disease that invaded her body, but nothing seemed to work. One by one Kathy's bodily systems began to shut down until one warm spring afternoon in April 1991, Kathy quietly died with her family and friends by her side. She was thirty-two years old.

I remember standing in the back of her hospital room, silently praying and weeping with tears running down my cheeks as the doctor disconnected her life support systems and pronounced Kathy dead. This awful tragedy dashed all our hopes for her recovery. I felt privileged to be with my friend and her family at the end of her short yet remarkable life, but incredibly sad at the loss of the most courageous person I have ever known.

While Kathy may have succumbed to the treatment for her leukemia, she left a lasting legacy. She was the reason four hundred and forty hospital employees, their families, and people in the community came forward, became educated, and made the commitment to put their names on the National Bone Marrow Donor Registry. Kathy started a trend in Central Ohio that continues to live today.

The evening the bone marrow drive concluded, Kathy and John took Mary, me, and several others involved in making the drive so successful, to dinner. We were all exhausted, none more so than Kathy, but we felt we had been part of something much bigger than ourselves. After dinner, as people were hugging and saying goodbye. Kathy quietly slipped cards to Mary and me and thanked us for our efforts. Inside my card, Kathy wrote, "You made me believe in miracles." Inside Mary's card, she wrote, "You have restored my faith in the human race." I still have that card today, almost thirty years since she placed it in my hand.

I think of Kathy often and wonder if she would make a different decision if she had to do it again. I have concluded, she would not. Kathy loved life, and the people in her life, especially her husband, and she wanted to hold on to that for as long as possible. Two or three additional years was much too short a period for a woman with her zest for living. She made the courageous decision to seek the ultimate cure and paid for it with her life. But I believe it was a debt she was willing to pay and one which has disbursed abundant dividends to her family, friends, and those afflicted with diseases that can be treated with bone marrow transplants.

Kathy took the ultimate chance, and in losing her life, she educated hundreds of people who are now in a position to give hope and time to others who are confronting the same fear and uncertainty that Kathy faced. In deciding to choose life over a few years of not dying, she displayed a type of courage rarely seen today.

I miss her happy face but smile when I think of the impact she had on the lives of others, including mine.

There are countless stories of people throughout history who have "failed" on numerous occasions only to succeed with another try. I have only listed a few within this chapter. However, I would guess that those successful individuals wouldn't look at their ineffective experiences as failures. They would not see the roadblock as a derailment of their dream. They would view them as opportunities to learn and move their idea in another direction.

But to fail, you have to take that first step. You have to be willing to move outside your comfort zone and do the things you may not want to do, or that scare you. If you aren't ready to take that chance and be an active participant in your idea, you won't fail, but neither will you have any hope of succeeding.

Waiting for the perfect set of circumstances to take your chance will cause tremendous consternation, because the ideal time will never present itself. The precise time to pursue your dreams is now (provided the risks you are taking have been calculated, and you aren't throwing your ideas against the wall in the hope that they stick).

We all know people who think or study things to death and are never able to pull the trigger and execute. It goes back to our brains not wanting us to fail or look bad. As a result, these people never get anything accomplished. **WE** are our most significant impediment to our success. Ben Franklin got it right when he said, "By failing to prepare, you are preparing to fail."

Failing doesn't have to be the end of the road. With the right attitude, it could be the start of the most rewarding portion of your life.

PRINCIPLE #9 – LISTEN MORE THAN YOU TALK

Always try to understand what is motivating others.

STEVEN R. COVEY HIT THE NAIL ON THE HEAD WHEN HE SAID, "SEEK first to understand, then to be understood."

I'm reminded of the Bible verse from 1 Kings 19:12 that expressly discusses the importance of actively listening, as God speaks to Elijah. The text is as follows:

Then the Lord said, "Go out and stand on the mountain before the Lord. Behold, the Lord is about to pass by." And a great and mighty wind tore into the mountains and shattered the rocks before the Lord, but the Lord was not in the wind. After the wind, there was an earthquake, but the Lord was not in the earthquake. After the earthquake, there was a fire, but the Lord was not in the fire. And after the fire came a still, small voice. And when Elijah heard it, he wrapped his face in his cloak and went out and stood at the mouth of the cave. Suddenly a voice came to him and said, "What are you doing here, Elijah?"

Some of the most potent forces on earth passed before Elijah: tornadic winds, a rumbling earthquake, and an inferno of fire surrounded him. The power of the earth is where you would expect God to present himself. But God was not in the power. God was not in the earth. God was in the still, small voice, almost a whisper. I've often wondered with all the technology and distractions we are exposed to every day, how would the formidable, but barely audible, Word of God ever reach us?

It seems the only way we can hear God speaking within our hearts, is to quiet ourselves and tune in to what is said. If that is what we need to do to understand the Creator of the universe, wouldn't it make sense that we should do the same with the people around us?

When I first started working, I was given two of the best pieces of advice I ever received. The first one was this: "Listen more than you talk. But don't listen to respond. Listen to understand where the other person is coming from." The second piece of advice was, "You were given two ears and one mouth for a reason." Years later, I found a quote from Abraham Lincoln that paralleled this guidance. The quote was this: "Better to remain silent and be thought a fool than to speak out and remove all doubt."

I became a Cincinnati Police Officer when I was thirty-seven years old. By most standards that is old to enter the field of law enforcement. But just like my basketball playing days, I wanted to be associated with the best. To me, that meant attempting to become a member of the Cincinnati Police Department's (CPD) SWAT team. The CPD SWAT team was made up of two groups that worked together. One group was the tactical team, and the other was the hostage/crisis negotiators.

When an opening became available for the negotiators, I signed up. I passed the physical fitness test, the psychological exam, and the interviews and was eventually selected to be one of the negotiators.

Being a hostage negotiator was one of the most enjoyable and rewarding jobs I experienced as a police officer.

Hostage/crisis negotiating is unique because we are attempting to deal with a person in crisis, but they aren't with us. Often, we were several blocks away from the person we were talking with due to safety considerations. Since we are unable to observe the physical cues their presence would provide us, we became experts at understanding people based on what they are saying, what they aren't saying, and how they are saying it.

The best way I can explain what we did as negotiators is with a teeter-totter example. We have all had the experience as children of playing on a teeter-totter at the park. When we start talking with a person in crisis, their teeter-totter's emotional end is high in the air, and their teeter-totter's rational side is on the ground. Over time, sometimes many hours, our goal is to bring the teeter-totter to equilibrium. Hopefully by the end of our negotiations, their teeter-totter's rational side is high in the air, and the emotional side is on the ground.

It wasn't until the individual could "bleed off" their emotional energy that we could begin discussing rational solutions to their crisis like coming out or freeing the hostage. This process involved a lot of "active listening." We wanted the person to talk as much as possible. At the same time, we asked open-ended questions and attempted to assign specific emotions or feelings to what we were hearing.

According to the National Council of Negotiation Associates, hostage/crisis negotiators bring a safe, peaceful, and non-violent conclusion to about 80% of the callouts to which they respond. When we were successful at bringing resolution to the incident, it was said that we "talked someone out." We didn't *talk* anyone out. Most of what we did was *listen* to what was being said and how it was being told. We then attempted to parrot back the thought with an emotion attached to it. If anything, we "listened people out."

I think you have to come into the negotiator position with some intuitiveness, but we trained every month by running through different scenarios and bouncing different solutions among our group. The more you experience people in crisis, and the more you understand the science behind how and why they are acting a certain way, the easier it is to be a good negotiator.

An essential skill we possessed wasn't our ability to talk; it was our ability to listen and understand what the person in crisis said. Armed with that information, we could work with them to hopefully end the situation in a peaceful manner. Most of the time, that is how these crises resolved themselves.

Unfortunately, no matter how hard we worked, there were times when the individual couldn't see a reasonable solution to the situation and decided to end their life. Those circumstances were always tragic, but I never lost any sleep over the events. I knew I had excellent training and worked with a group of negotiators who did their best to resolve these very chaotic situations successfully.

I didn't put the person in crisis in this situation. Many times, their issues had been years in the making, and we did our best to attempt to resolve the situation in a matter of hours peacefully. Often, that just wasn't realistic, but we always did our best to listen to what the person was communicating.

Effectively communicating is one of the most important skills we can learn. I remember, as a child, the different riddles we were always asked in school. A few of my favorites were: "You are the engineer of a train. You leave the station with 125 passengers. At the first stop, 25 passengers depart, and 12 more get on the train. At the next stop, 45 people get off, and 22 people embark. When you reach your final destination at the next station, what is the engineer's age?" Since I said that *you* are the engineer, the answer would be *your* age.

I had a grade-school teacher who loved the magician Harry Houdini. She used to give us magician riddles. The one I liked the most went like this: "One day, a magician was boasting how long he could hold his breath underwater. He said his record was five minutes. A boy that was listening said, 'That's nothing; I can stay underwater for ten minutes.' Not wanting to be upstaged by a child, the magician bet the boy $100 that he couldn't do what he said he could. The young boy did it and won the money. How did this boy accomplish such a remarkable feat? The answer was, he filled a glass with water and held it over his head for ten minutes."

This riddle is so simple that it was all over my high school growing up. It went like this: "What comes once in a minute, twice in a moment, but never in a thousand years?" The answer was the letter *M*.

To prove the importance of listening, I vividly recall my seventh grade English teacher giving us these verbal instructions before a test. She said, "Before starting the test, make sure you read the directions carefully and do what they say." Being in a hurry to complete the exam, I didn't take the time to read the instructions and started right in answering the questions. After answering the first question, I was puzzled as to why several of my classmates were turning in their tests. There was no way they could have finished this two-page exam so quickly. After about thirty minutes, I was confident I had answered all the questions correctly and turned in my exam. After giving it to my teacher, smug in the satisfaction that I did well on the exam, she took it and wrote a big *F* at the top of my paper and handed it back to me. When I asked her why I had failed the exam, she said, "Because you didn't read the directions." As I took the paper and made my way back to my seat, I couldn't understand what she was saying. I was so focused on how much I studied and how well I answered the questions that her reason for failing me still hadn't registered. It wasn't until I was back at my desk that I took the time to read the instructions. Here is what they said: "This is a pass/fail test. You will either receive an *A* or an *F* as a grade. To get an *A* on the test, write your name, in cursive, on the line at the top of the paper next to the word *Name*: and turn in the test. If you answer any of the other questions on this test, you will receive the grade of *F*. I felt like such an idiot for not listening to what the teacher had told us at the beginning of the test. By not actively listening to the instructions, I turned an easy *A* into a failing grade.

Depending on the topic of the presentation I am giving, I will sometimes end the talk by asking the audience to do me a favor. I ask them to spend one day with someone close to them and try to understand what is being said during a conversation. When the person finishes speaking, I ask them to pause, rephrase in their mind what the person just said, and attach an emotion to the words. After they have done that, they can respond to the person.

Without a doubt, the feedback I receive about this exercise helps people better understand what is being said and the feeling with which the remarks are being communicated.

Listening to understand, instead of being understood, will make you a better communicator and make you a better conversationalist.

PRINCIPLE #10 – LOVE IS THE MOST IMPORTANT WORD IN ANY LANGUAGE

Love yourself, love the people in your life, but most importantly, love the people who don't deserve your love, they need it the most.

LOVE IS NOT A WORD YOU HEAR A LOT THESE DAYS. WE SEEM TO BE always tearing each other down as a way of lifting ourselves up. So, love doesn't easily come off the lips of too many people in our current culture.

When I was being taught about my Catholic faith, I learned that our God was three persons in one God. Those three persons were the Father, the Son, and the Holy Spirit. During my preparation for the Confirmation sacrament, I was taught that I would be receiving the Holy Spirit's gifts. But who or what was the Holy Spirit? You could understand a Father figure, and it was readily understood what a Son was. But what was the Holy Spirit? The name almost sounded like some form of ghost or apparition. As a youngster, the Holy Spirit sounded scary and uninviting. For me, the Holy Spirit seemed disconnected from the Holy Trinity.

I learned in Confirmation class that the Holy Spirit was the *love* that the Father has for the Son and that the Son reciprocates to the Father. The Holy Spirit wasn't a frightening entity. It was anything but. It was the love shared between the two other members of the Holy Trinity.

While that understanding answered one question, it begged another. What is love? When Roberta and I were married, one of the wedding gifts we received was a framed plaque with the Bible verse from 1 Corinthians 13:4-8. The verse answers the question, what is love. It goes like this:

> *"Love is patient, love is kind. It does not envy, it does not boast, it is not proud. It does not dishonor others, it is not self-liking, it is not easily angered, it keeps no record of wrongs. Love does not delight in evil but rejoices in the truth. It always protects, always trusts, always hopes, always perseveres. Love never fails. But where there are prophecies, they will cease; where there are tongues, they will be stilled; where there is knowledge, it will pass away."*

But other than a Bible verse, what does love look like from a practical sense? Are there any concrete examples of how love manifests itself? Were there instances that you would immediately know were the action of love if you saw them?

I remember reading a story from the Vatican about a man who was dubbed the Saint of Auschwitz, Maximilian Kolbe. His story is one that I think most people would look at as a perfect example of love.

Raymond Kolbe was born in 1894 in Poland. As a young boy, he had a vision of Mary, the Blessed Mother, who asked him to choose between a red and a white crown. The white crown represented purity, and the red one signified martyrdom. He couldn't make a singular choice, so he decided to take both.

From an early age, Raymond knew his vocation was to be in the religious life. After joining the Franciscan Order and being given the name Maximillian, he began his studies in Poland. He was sent to

Rome in 1912 to continue his schooling and was ordained a priest in 1918.

Having returned to Poland, Maximillian and a few of the priests, organized a temporary hospital at the beginning of World War II. He was initially arrested in 1939 by the Germans after they invaded Poland but was released several months later.

In February 1941, he was arrested by the Gestapo and sent to the Auschwitz Concentration Camp. Father Kolbe continued to perform his role as a priest and was beaten and tortured for his Catholic beliefs and actions at Auschwitz.

In July 1941, a prisoner escaped from Auschwitz. To deter further escape attempts, the deputy camp commander chose ten prisoners to starve to death. One of the men selected cried out that he had a wife and children. Father Kolbe's request to take the man's place was granted.

The ten men were led to an underground bunker. Every day Father Kolbe led the men in prayer. After two weeks, Maximillian was the only person who remained alive. The guards wanted the bunker emptied, so they gave Father Kolbe a deadly injection of carbolic acid. It is reported that Father Kolbe raised his left arm and waited for the lethal injection. He died on August 14, 1941.

Father Kolbe's self-sacrifice, out of love for his fellow man, is saintly and virtuous. As a result of his actions, he was canonized as a saint by Pope John Paul II on October 10, 1982.

Maximillian Kolbe is a perfect example of the quote from John's gospel, *"Greater love has no man than this, that he lay down his life for his friend."*

While most of us would like to think we are saintly, we are just regular people trying to do the right things, at the right time, for the right reasons. The vast majority of us will never be beatified a saint by a pope.

So, what does love look like for us mere mortals? Matthew Danuser and Disty Simpson wanted to help others in their hometown of Oklahoma City. So, they went to a location that all of us go to every week, the grocery store.

After receiving permission from the store manager, they would identify people who were shopping, get behind them at the check-out line, and once all the groceries were scanned, they would step in and pay the bill. Sometimes they would pay for a gallon of milk. Other times they would purchase an entire cart full of food.

To start a movement of people helping others, they videotaped their exploits and uploaded them to the internet. Very quickly, they had over fourteen million views, and donations began to pour in.

A simple act of kindness has led to a worldwide movement called Fill My Basket. This humble act of love has generated millions of dollars and spawned affiliates across the country.

When Roberta and I were preparing to be married in the Catholic Church, we were required to attend a Pre-Cana course to ensure we had discussed such topics as conflict resolution, finances, intimacy, faith, children, and commitment. The Pre-Cana name is derived from the Gospel of John 2: 1-12, the wedding at Cana, where Jesus performed the miracle of turning water into wine.

As part of this course, we were required to study specific readings and stories and discuss them during a weekly meeting with each other and the priest. One of the stories was as follows:

"There was a blind boy who resented his disability and was mean and nasty to everyone he met. He had no friends, and even his family despised being in his presence because he was so cruel.

One day, a young girl transferred into the class with the blind boy. She initially tried to make small talk with him, but he shunned her kindness like everyone else. Undeterred, the girl continued to be caring to the blind boy. After months of her affection, the boy relented, and the two went on a date. After several dates, they became a couple, and after many months of courtship, the boy said he would marry the girl if only he could see her.

As fortune would have it, a pair of eyes were donated, and the boy was the lucky recipient of the eyes. Shortly after the bandages were removed, the boy was able to gaze on the beautiful face of the girl he said he would marry. However, to his astonishment, he realized she was blind. She asked him, 'Since you can see me now, when can we be married?'

The boy replied that the marriage would not work out. He had his sight, but she was still blind. They would never be happily married.

Saddened, the girl turned to leave and said she just wanted him to be happy. 'Take care of yourself,' she said, 'and my eyes.'"

The moral of this story is that love causes people to give of themselves to those they care about. In this case, the girl loved the boy so much that she was willing to give her sight so that he could see. However, the selfishness of the boy prevented him from seeing the tremendous gift he had been given and he just assumed the marriage wouldn't work because his partner was blind. I've often wondered what the boy thought when he realized the girl, out of pure love, had given him her gift of sight.

As I've mentioned previously, athletics, specifically basketball, was an essential part of my life. Basketball was probably *the* most important part of my life. It was so prominent that I have often felt that my commitment to the game caused me to be selfish and more concerned with what I needed to do to be a better basketball player, instead of showing a greater interest in the people around me.

John Wooden, the hall of fame basketball coach at UCLA, was considered the greatest coach in the sport when I was growing up. His teams were so dominant that they won ten NCAA national championships in twelve years, including a record seven in a row.

Within that period, his teams won an NCAA men's basketball record of 88 consecutive games.

But for all his excellence on the basketball court, Coach Wooden was probably noted for something even more impressive, his Pyramid of Success. The Pyramid of Success consists of the building blocks that outline the philosophy of succeeding in life.

I heard an interview given by Coach Wooden, where he was asked what the most important word in any language was. Coach Wooden was quick to respond that the most important word in any language was love.

One of the most successful coaches in sports history was boiling excellence into a single word—love.

The love that God has for each of us, the unconditional love in which we were created, is the most important gift we have ever been given and that we can give to others. We can't do anything to make God love us more, and we can't do anything to make him love us less. God knew every sin we would commit. He knew all our faults and transgressions, and yet He still loved us enough to want us to be born. His absolute and unqualified love for each of us provides us the grace to freely accept His love, categorically love Him in return, and, maybe more importantly, love the people we don't believe deserve our love.

EPILOGUE

IN THINKING ABOUT THE BIG PICTURE OF YOUR LIFE, WHAT WILL BE THE one point that stands out about you and that will be discussed at the eulogy of your funeral? What will your legacy be? Will people say you died before you were dead, or will they speak about how much you will be missed because you were a person of integrity who tried to live a principle-centered life?

I'm reminded of the final scene in the mini-series *Band of Brothers*. In this scene, all the soldiers who served in Easy Company were individually singled out and highlighted for what they did after the war. The paratrooper I always remember from this scene was George Luz. It was said that after the war, George became a handyman in Providence, Rhode Island. As a testament to his character, sixteen hundred people attended his funeral in 1998.

You were born to live an uncommon and extraordinary life. But to accomplish that, you have to be committed to a life based on a set of principles that will allow you to exist in a virtuous way without letting your emotions dictate your behavior. You need to control your mind. You need to embrace the pain and suffering you will experience. You need to do the things that scare you and that you don't want to do. You always need to keep moving forward and continuously remind yourself that as long as you don't quit, you can never be defeated.

Stuart Scott, the ESPN sportscaster who died of cancer in 2015, is reported to have said, "Don't downgrade your dreams to fit your reality, upgrade your convictions to match your destiny."

If you want to live that uncommon and extraordinary life, you have to upgrade your convictions. If your destiny is predicated on how you react emotionally instead of principally, you will never realize your life's fulfillment.

I chose the ten principles in this book based on the mistakes I have made in my life and the challenges I have overcome. I spent too much of my life attempting to live my father's life instead of the life I was born to live. My father's motives were pure and based on love and what he believed was in my best interest. But his version of my life was not the life God called me to live.

I let the emotions of fear and insecurity cloud so many of my decisions before I realized I was better off making my mind think with the realization that I was strong enough to handle whatever pitfalls might come my way as a result of those thoughts.

Living an uncommon and extraordinary life was something I thought I was doing until I understood the only way I could be successful or improve myself was to face my fears and insecurities head-on. The act of confronting my adversity is what made me stronger and better.

Curiosity has always been one of my strong suits. It is what helped me to be a competent police officer. People and their journeys fascinate me. It used to drive Roberta crazy when we would go to a party, and I would spend the evening working the room and came away knowing quite a bit about the lives of the people at the party, but they knew almost nothing about me. People are narcissistic and love to talk about themselves. If you want to be a great conversationalist, just ask people about themselves and be quiet. I also knew I was never the smartest person, but I could learn from others.

It was always more comfortable for me to let others make decisions for me. Beginning with college and going through my first two jobs, I allowed my father to influence my course of study and where I would work. You become your own person when you can make decisions for yourself and live with the consequences of those decisions. Those decisions aren't always easy, but the difficult ones allowed me to grow and mature.

God was one of those principles that were offered to me at an early age. However, thinking I was stronger than I was, I didn't commit to Him as early as I should. But as I grew into a man, I realized that, no matter how strong I perceived myself to be, I wasn't able to ford the rapids of life on my own. I was put here for a reason and by a God that loved me unconditionally. Why wouldn't I use His power to determine where I needed to go and how I was going to get there? My life went great when I relied on Him and not so great when I relied solely on me. As my life draws to a close, I'm not afraid of death and am almost excited about what the next journey has in store. God put that excitement in my heart, and he can put it in you no matter how much you've disregarded His word or what obstacles you are facing in your life.

My happiest times have been when I was working with others to accomplish something that we weren't sure we could complete. Or when you knew another human being was reliant upon you for all their needs in the world, and they looked up to you as though you were larger than life. Those are the times you feel alive, and as though you have a purpose.

I have failed many times in my life, but I never failed enough. That's because I was thinking with my fears and insecurities, and my mind stopped me from trying new things that, even if I had failed, would have made me a better person. I played it safe way too much, especially when I was starting in my career. I should have lived my life, even if it meant I would have failed.

I am a great talker. I can talk to anybody about anything at any time. But for a long time, I wasn't a great listener. At least not a big listener when it came to listening to understand instead of listening to reply. I listened a lot with the singular purpose of putting my two cents into the conversation. I became a better police officer when I learned to listen to understand. That made me a better person, husband, and father. It also made me a better crisis/hostage negotiator.

I've said previously that your life should be based on principles instead of emotions. I believe that is true except for the essential item we all need in our lives, and that item just happens to be an emotion, the emotion of love. I'm not talking about romantic love; that fades over time, and what you're left with is true love. And true love, sacrificing self for others, is the MOST IMPORTANT thing in our world. It is what caused us to be created. While it is important to love ourselves, it is even more critical (and harder) to love others. Especially those who are "different" than us. Everybody you meet was created out of God's love to fulfill a unique and special role. No two people who have ever been born are alike. Let that sink in. Nobody who ever was born or whoever will be born is like you. Your gifts and talents, given to you by God, make you unique. When you can appreciate your uniqueness, you will understand the real meaning of Love.

How you live your life today will depend on two things, not allowing yourself to make decisions solely based on emotions and tying the principles you hold to the beliefs you have in your heart. No matter where you are, no matter how far down you may be, you can start from there and rise like a phoenix from the ashes of your own making.

If you can apply the principles in this book to every minute of your day, you will be well on your way to a life of sustainable excellence. A life that may not be understood by others but a life that will allow you to be true to yourself, to your heart, and your God. And when your life is concluded, you will be able to stand in the presence of our Creator and be able to account for the gifts you were given at birth and how you used them to live your uncommon and extraordinary life and make His world a better place.

I think that will be the true meaning of heaven.

I'd like to close with the following story that my father had framed and hanging in his home office. It is a story that I have read hundreds of times throughout my life. It is a story that helped me set my personal compass and taught me about the principle of never giving up. It is a story that has brought me peace. I hope it brings the same to you. The story is entitled: *What a Father Says to His Son before his First Game.* The author is unknown.

"This is your first game, son. I hope you win for your sake, not mine. Because winning is nice. It's a good feeling. Like the whole world is yours. But it passes, this feeling. And what lasts is what you've learned. And what you learn about is life. That is what competition is all about. Life. The whole thing is played out in one afternoon. The happiness of life. The miseries. The joy. The heartbreaks. There is no telling what will turn up. There is no telling whether they will toss you out in the first five minutes or whether you will stay for the long haul. There is just no telling how you will do. You might be a hero, or you might be absolutely nothing. There is just no telling. Too much depends on chance. On how the ball bounces. I'm not talking about the game, son. I'm talking about life. But it's life that the game is all about. Just as I said. Because every game is life. And life is a game. A serious one. Dead serious! But that's what you do with serious things. You do your best. You take what comes. You take what comes and run with it. Winning is fun, sure. But winning is not the point. Wanting to win is the point. Never giving up is the point. Never being satisfied with what you have done is the point. Never letting up is the point. Never letting anyone down is the point. Play to win, sure. But lose like a champion. Because it's not winning that counts. What counts is trying."

You can commit to every one of these principles and make them part of who you are, an uncommon and extraordinary person. You have the ability, but do you have the mental toughness to incorporate these principles into your soul? The question is, will you use these principles to lead your uncommon or extraordinary life, or will you settle for a life of the ordinary and typical? The choice is yours.

ACKNOWLEDGMENTS

Writing a book is more challenging than I thought and more gratifying than I could ever imagine. This book would have never been possible without all the people listed below:

Thanks to Scott and Leah Silverii and everyone at Five Stones Press, including my amazing and talented editors: Imogen Howsen, Kimberly Cannon & Ava Hodge, and Wicked Smart Design for their incredible cover art and everyone involved who took this jumble of words and turned it into a purposeful book.

Thanks to Nancy Schlichting, Gene Henneberry, and Colleen Durbin Mitchell for their willingness to take time from their busy schedules to not only read the manuscript and provide me with cover quotes but also give me feedback to make the book even better.

Thanks to Jonathan & Logan Aal for the time they took to read the first draft and provide me with comments and help me realize that this book could have meaning and purpose to those who read it.

Thanks to my immediate and extended family for their love and constant support: my wife Roberta, our daughter Mikela (and her fiancé Bret Herring), my mother, Marilyn, my brothers Larry (Anne) and Bryan, my Uncle David (Bud) Muckle, my cousins: David Muckle, Mary Bennett, Diane Middleton, Terry Campbell, and Lisa Muckle, my nephew and nieces: Ryan Tucker, Maddie Tucker, Lauren Tucker, and Jaclyn Tucker, my in-laws: Dale & Wendy Thompson, Jeff Olson, and Randy Olson.

Thanks to everyone in Houston who supported our family when the greatest challenge of my life occurred in 2012: Dr. Jade Schiffman (the sister I never had) and her late father and dear friend, Bud, Danielle Resh, Taylor Bookstaff, Dr. Steve Sax, Shane & April Burgin, and everyone who provided us with meals, love, and support.

Thanks to our Denver area friends who sustained our family through countless crises and surgeries: Brian & Angela Dziubek, Tim & Holly Wieser, Larry & Julie Koornneef, Lisa & Todd Glanzer, Gary Bartel, Gino Vella, Jim & Pam Whiteside, Gibson & Laurie Smith, Eric & Lindsay Bernum, Colleen Denzler & her husband, Scott Allen, and Pat Welsh, Steven Kruse, and Leslie Monaco.

Thanks to my lifelong friends, The Henneberry Family, Jim Kent, Bill Baker, George Splawski, Kim & Damon Pendarvis, Ron Hale, Christine Briede, Joan & Fred Manter, Diane Blackwelder, Micki Browning, Mary McRury, Dianne O'Brien, Jennifer, Wilford, Mary Alice Bletzacker, Aaron Turbett, Allen Eggert, Lynn Jeffrey, Sam Miglarese, Richard Johnson, Jette McDonald, John Mackessy, Scott Funk, and Jerry Savage.

Thanks to my medical teams at MD Anderson Cancer Center in Houston and the University of Colorado Cancer Center - Anschutz Campus in Denver: Dr. Sapna Patel, Dr. Scott Oates, Dr. Karl Lewis, Dr. Martin McCarter, Dr. Andrew Park, Dr. Daniel Moon, Dr. Misha Miller, Dr. Lavanya Kondapalli, Dr. Justin Merkow, Dr. Max Wohlauer, Dr. Katherine Payne, Physical Therapist Brian Anobile, Physical Therapist Lee Bernhardt, Occupational Therapist Erin Erickson and all the outstanding nurses, therapists, and technicians who provided me with such quality and compassionate care.

And finally, thanks to Alexa, for providing me with the correct spelling of so many words in this book!

ABOUT THE AUTHOR

Terry Tucker has been an NCAA Division I college basketball player, a Citadel cadet, an undercover narcotics investigator, a SWAT Team Hostage Negotiator, a high school basketball coach, a business owner, and most recently, a cancer warrior.

He and his wife have lived all over the United States and currently reside in Colorado with their daughter and Wheaten Terrier, Maggie.

In 2019 , Terry started the website, Motivational Check, to help others find and lead their uncommon and extraordinary lives. More information and his podcasts can be found at motivationalcheck.com.

CPSIA information can be obtained
at www.ICGtesting.com
Printed in the USA
LVHW080845191020
669145LV00023B/181/J

9 781951 129521